THE WISDOM
OF LISTENING

PIECES OF GOLD FROM A DECADE
OF INTERVIEWING AND LIFE

MARILYN R. WILSON

Editing: Nina Shoroplova

Typeset: Greg Salisbury

Author Image: Photographer Eydis Einarsdottir

Original Artwork (cover) —Listen to the silence underneath the sounds by Sabina Sýkorová (Blue-birch-insight)

Artwork Adaptation and Book Cover Design—Adrian Horvath

DISCLAIMER: This is a work of non-fiction. The information in this book reflects interviews that were carried out by the author. Readers of the publication agree that neither Marilyn R. Wilson, nor her imprint,

BODY, MIND & SPIRIT/Inspiration & Personal Growth
SELF-HELP/Motivational & Inspirational
SELF-HELP/Personal Growth/Self-Esteem

Testimonials

"Marilyn listens with her 'heart'... she hears even your silence."
Denise Brillon, Designer/Producer

"Reading The Wisdom of Listening *was a great comfort as I was reminded we are collectively each walking our own paths, but often experience similar emotions, feelings, obstacles, challenges, triumphs, rewards and successes. We all learn as we go and we all become wiser as time passes. This is humanity. The diversity in each of us as a whole is awesome."*
RozeMerie Cuevas, Co-Founder and Designer at JAC by Jacqueline Conoir

"I love how Marilyn has woven her own aha moments into her interviews, delivering timeless messages about life, love, compassion, self-acceptance and healing. Every life has a story, and no matter our background, we share similar hopes, dreams and fears. This book not only gives you insight into the varied lives of its subjects, but through Marilyn's reflections, shows how we each walk a similar spiritual path, and we truly learn about ourselves when we learn about each other. It's been wonderful to learn more about Marilyn."
Robbin Whachell, Founder and Editor-in-Chief of The Bahamas Weekly

"PowHERful nuggets of inspiration provide tangible evidence that the Universe is alive and well in our daily lives. Hits of insight and guidance are regularly delivered to us from a Higher Source through our conversations when we connect and listen, really listen, to those we interact with both personally and professionally. Thank you, Marilyn, for demonstrating these lessons so powHERfully!"
Charlene SanJenko, PowHERhouse Media Group

"Marilyn Wilson is an incredible soul with limitless gifts. When her words hit paper they always come to life! A prolific writer, style icon and devoted mother and wife whose writing is both inspiring and relevant."
Warren Dean Flandez, Award Winning Recording Artist, Founder of Studio Cloud 30

"Marilyn has the gift of storytelling. Her animated yet warm personality is authentic and compassionate as are her words and her wisdom. Over the years, I have had the honor of being interviewed by her and now we have established a meaningful lifelong friendship. For the first time, she shares her story and reveals her powerful connection to storytelling, how it not only has transformed her life but that of others as well."
Katherine Soucie, Designer, Sans Soucie Textile + Design (Eco Fashion Line), Artist and Educator

"Marilyn, you could not have spoken better words in your book. This book is powerful and I highly recommend it to people who are crying out for positive, loving, supportive guidance in their life. There's no need to pretend who you are anymore. Give your life energy through your wardrobe, success and the beauty that lies within!"
Jo Hausman, Speaker, Radio Talk Show Host, Best Selling Author and Coach

"*Marilyn Wilson has a unique ability to pull out the golden nuggets from the people she interviews. This book is the culmination of all those magical golden moments woven into her own story, and how each person deeply touched and influenced the way she lives her life. These inspiring short stories will touch your life and influence the way you go through life. I can guarantee you'll be repeating these golden nuggets and touching the lives of many.*"
Julie Salisbury, Founder of Influence Publishing and InspireABook

"*Marilyn weaves the stories of others in with her own to create a masterpiece of inspiration that is The Wisdom of Listening. Each share, each story, each fiber of the weave serves to remind us that we are not alone in our journey, and that the human spirit triumphs over life's inevitable knock-outs. A must read!*"
Krylyn Peters, Host of Get Out of Your Own Damn Way Podcast

"*Everyone should dig into this for you will strike gold at every turn. As I journeyed with you in your stories, Marilyn, my journey was unfolding right alongside. I was simply reeling in every word. Within every word was another story and a vibration that struck a chord. It's as if you spoke to me directly, sharing your wisdom to give me wisdom.*"
Steely Springham, Confidence Coach, Certified Behaviour Change Specialist, Speaker and Canadian National Figure & Fitness Athlete

"*The Wisdom of Listening is amazing and touching. Very authentic and real. I have known Marilyn for several years and heard some of these pieces of gold before. Reading this book is like she is right here in the room with me sharing them again, but in more detail.*"
Angela Krewenchuk, Founder of Metro Living Zine Agency

"*The Wisdom of Listening reminds us we need to stop, take it slow, listen with head and heart as the author does, for the golden nuggets in every gesture and in every spoken dream. Marilyn shows us, through her compassionate and incisive interviews, how to grasp and link those golden moments, like sparkling prisms of light, into an animated and profound acceptance of ourselves, the people we encounter, the relationships we build, and the dreams that will set us free.*"
Gabriella Contestabile, Author of Sass, Smarts, and Stilettos: How Italian Women Make the Ordinary Extraordinary , Founder of Su Misura Sensory Journeys

"*Marilyn is a talented and passionate woman who loves life and all those who surround her as seen in her writings.*""
Paul Mantello, Author and Life Success Coach, Author of Transform Your Life, Business & Health

Contents

Acknowledgements

Too many people have encouraged, supported and mentored me on my journey the last two years to mention everyone. For some it takes just one or two people to help them realize their dreams. For me, on the other hand, it seems to take a village and I'm happy with that arrangement.

There are, however, several I would like to take a moment and mention as their support was crucial in making this book a reality.

To my husband Glen—Thanks for always having my back. You stand behind me without question and give me the freedom and space to do what I need to do. I am filled with gratitude every day for this gift.

To my lovely daughter Danielle—You have a gift when it comes to the English language that always amazes me. Thanks for stepping in and offering guidance. You are my personal secret weapon.

To my publisher and friend Julie Salisbury—You have held my hand from day one in my journey to becoming a published author, always there to lift me up when I stumble and celebrate with me every time I reach a new milestone. If I had never met you, my life would be very different.

To my gifted editor Nina Shoroplova—I am often asked

about the editing process and my answer always takes people by surprise. I let them know a good editor is not there to be your best buddy and tell you how fabulous you are. They are there to help you reach new heights as an author. Thanks for your honesty and the patient, kind touch with which you offer your guidance. I continue to grow as a writer because of you and hope we work together for years to come.

To my mentor Sue Dumais of Heart Led Living—You have guided me patiently for two years through many "unwindings" where I discovered the truth hidden beneath. It was through your guidance I came to understand this was the next book I needed to write. Many of your pieces of gold can be found within these pages and I am filled with gratitude that your heart answered yes to writing the foreword.

Last but never least, to my "ujamaa tribe" of wonderful friends—You stand behind me, give me the words of encouragement I need in difficult moments and raise me up when I falter. None of this would be possible without each and every one of you. I love you all.

"I like messy people; people who don't fit in a box or stay between the lines, but whose integrity is greater than any rule book and whose loyalty is stronger than blood."
Jim Wern, Blogger

Foreword

When a pebble is dropped into a vast body of water, its ripples extend seemingly forever. Our nuggets of wisdom have much of the same effect. They may seem to land in the heart of one or two, but really they are like pebbles, creating ripple effects that can't possibly be measured.

Imagine how different the world would be if we all made a commitment to listen more deeply. Listening is a gift for both the one who is speaking as well as the listener. What if more people gathered nuggets of wisdom and shared them with others as inspired? The insights would be passed on and on like ancient teachings.

The words would become expressions of love being extended outward reaching beyond all geographical boundaries. We would all feel a deeper connection to each other and the energy of love would rise. Love is what the world needs now more than ever, and love is what is infused in the pages of this book.

When I first met Marilyn at an event, she was fluttering around the room with an incredible energy and excitement for life. I could sense her strength, courage and determination to touch the hearts of many. I could feel her soul take full flight fueled by her passion and desire to be of service to others.

Over the years I have heard Marilyn share many of the gold nuggets of wisdom she has written about on the pages of this book. I was thrilled to hear she was following her heart's nudge to pause all other projects and write *The Wisdom of Listening*. When Marilyn asked if I felt inspired to write the foreword for this book, I immediately felt a huge heart YES!

Imparting wisdom is a passion of mine, and so is listening. I have learned to listen with all my senses, and as an intuitive healer this allows me to tap into a wisdom that goes beyond our limited minds into a source that is far greater and more far-reaching than we can imagine. I was actually surprised by how many times in this book Marilyn mentioned some words of wisdom I have shared with her and I am touched to hear how they have left such a strong imprint. It made me pause and reflect on just how much we can impact each other without even realizing it.

Marilyn is always listening; she is wildly intrigued by people and their stories. This book not only provides great insight but also offers a beautiful peek into the life of a passionate and caring woman who is a sponge for wisdom, connection and growth. Marilyn has a gift with words and provides a beautiful vehicle to impart wisdom through sharing stories.

Open your mind wide, listen with your inner ear and let the nuggets of wisdom land in your heart. Then be willing to pay it forward by sharing this book and the loving messages, insights and wisdom with others. It will take a village. Are you willing to play your part? This love-inspired action will change the world and raise the level of love, one heart at a time.

by Sue Dumais, Founder of Heart Led Living

"Until you spread your wings you will have no idea how far you can fly."
Unknown

Introduction

The Wisdom of Listening is a passion project that has been patiently waiting to be realized for some time. Each chapter stands alone, so this book does not have to be read the traditional way—from front to back. You can pick it up whenever you have free time and dive randomly into any chapter that interests you. The choice is yours.

Over my decade of interviewing, people have shared freely and honestly with me about their life journeys and the lessons they have learned along the way. During that same time my personal journey has also taught me a great deal. As much as I can, I pay this forward to those whose lives I have the privilege to touch.

In 2016 I was given a book to review that caught my imagination—*Giving Candy to Strangers* by Stan Holden. It was filled with short, one-idea chapters, some only a page or two long. I could read a chapter in the morning with my coffee and be left with an idea to ponder as I went through my day, or over the next week if I had a full schedule.

It quickly dawned on me that this format would be perfect for passing on some of the many bits of wisdom handed to me over the years. What a wonderful way to offer what I had learned—one small bite at a time.

The term "pieces of gold" arose during an intense interview with artist Pamela Masik. You will have the opportunity to read about this moment in an upcoming chapter, so I won't elaborate on it here. This phrase was and still is the best description I have found for what I receive during every interview and in my daily life.

Each of us has acquired wisdom on our personal journey, wisdom that's ready to be shared with others. They in return have wisdom ready to share with us.

My life of interviewing is an intuition-led, organic experience of both listening to others and sharing with them about myself—each an intimate conversation. No two are the same.

After listening to over a hundred and fifty unique people share their journeys from birth to where they are in that moment, I can guarantee you that real people sharing about their real lives is much more interesting than anything you'll ever see on reality television. You cannot help but be affected.

The gift of hearing such a wide variety of stories is truly life-changing; I know I will never be the same. And I believe with all my heart that it is the journey of real people living real lives that will define our generation.

Most of us love to express our own thoughts and ideas, so sharing with others is the easier part of the equation. More difficult for many of us is to stay silent and be present while others share, but I can promise you it's well worth the effort.

I have been brought to laughter and tears, heard the

most amazing stories and even been profoundly affected by listening to a random stranger met on a bus, a subway or in line for coffee. When the goosebumps occur, I know something important was just said.

You never know who will hand you that piece of gold you've been waiting for, and you never know whose life you will affect by sharing yours.

Be brave, be open, be willing, be curious.

- Marilyn R. Wilson

"Goosebumps: when your soul suddenly gets warmer
than your body."
Unknown

~

My Story

Why is it most people think their own story isn't very interesting? I run into this all the time when interviewing someone new. Unless they're a celebrity, a world traveler, an athlete, an award winner or someone who is somehow recognized by society's standards as a "success," they think they won't have enough to offer. This is never the case.

Over time one of my catch phrases has become, "Everyone has a story to tell. It's just a matter of asking the right questions." During an interview, the burden is on me to find a way to draw your story out and I have yet to be disappointed when I do.

I have over a hundred and fifty in-depth interviews under my belt and every single story has been worth hearing. Each offered me a new idea, a new way of looking at a problem or an interesting life-changing moment.

However, when I sat down to write my own story, it was hilarious to discover none of that mattered. I had those same feelings of "not enough" bubble up. I too find myself riddled with thoughts of being uninteresting when the tables are turned and I am being interviewed. I've lived every day of my life, so it honestly isn't all that interesting to me. Yet for some reason, others seem to feel what I share is worth hearing. Who knew?

So here it is, told as briefly as possible—my journey to interviewing and how profoundly my life has been affected by listening to so many share their truly unique and diverse life stories.

My father was a minister in a very small town in the Midwestern United States. My mother was a minister's wife, dedicated to supporting his work and the church. When a beautiful little blonde girl was born, they had visions of sugar and spice and everything nice. Unfortunately, I wasn't even "puppy-dogs tails."

I was bright, intense and my mind raced. I had no patience and I lost my temper easily. I was great at starting things but quickly lost interest, and I was always intensely curious about people (read: *nosy*). Not exactly what my parents had signed on for.

If our family had not had to live in a fishbowl surrounded by public opinion, I think this wouldn't have been as hard for all of us. The fact that they loved me was never in doubt, but I just wasn't capable of fitting into the role of "minister's daughter" that the congregation and my parents expected of me.

Unfortunately, they weren't able to hide the truth that who I was as a person hurt their ministry and brought them grief; my emotional radar for others has always been strong. In social settings, I could feel disapproval emanate toward me from across the room.

I grew up feeling like I was standing outside the house

looking in through the front window at a happy family spending time together. Everyone else seemed to be able to pull it off. What was wrong with me? Why couldn't I fit myself in the box? I felt like I was broken. With no answer forthcoming, the anger and hurt slowly built.

During my teen years this struggle extended into the rest of my life. It was difficult to fit in as—unlike other girls my age—I didn't go through the boy-crazy, celebrity-idol-worship phase. I was way more intense than my classmates and I chose to channel my frustrations into the problems I saw in the world—the Vietnam War, civil rights, inequities, poverty. Anyone around me who was suffering took center stage.

I will always be grateful to my friends Randi, Pat and Linda for being there. Having three people to eat lunch with and just hang out with at school helped ease the emotional burden I carried. Unfortunately there was no internet when I graduated, so we quickly lost touch. Thankfully, social media allowed us to reconnect a few years ago.

No one was surprised when I chose to graduate a year early and head off to university. Psychology drew me like a moth to a flame. My personal struggles and strong empathy for others made it a natural choice.

I envisioned a future where I would be helping clients with their pain and making a real difference in their lives. Obviously they would be grateful and I would have value. As a side benefit, many of the courses I was taking helped me look more clearly at my own personal struggles.

3

A few years after completing my bachelor's degree, I started the next step—earning my master's degree in Counselling and Drug Abuse, a degree that led mostly into marriage, family and child counselling. Working on a master's degree is very different from earning a bachelor's degree. Students are more focused and committed. Classroom discussions are at a different level—not as much about theory and more about application. For the first time I found myself totally inspired and earned honors in each and every course.

One night everything shifted.

My teacher had his own private practice. In an intense classroom moment he shared how two of his clients had committed suicide in the previous year, and that he was currently counselling a father who was struggling with sexual feelings toward his teenage daughter.

Then came the most damning remark. Marriage, family and child counselors usually only experience a positive outcome—couples staying together, family rifts healing—with five percent of their clients. People often come to counselors as a last resort, as a way to show they tried. Unfortunately for most, permanent damage to the relationship has already been done.

For a few seconds I couldn't breathe. I wanted to do something positive in the world. I wanted to help people. This path had seemed the right direction for so many years, yet in this moment it suddenly became crystal clear that psychology was not the right career for me. I would never be able to leave all that emotional baggage at the office or deal with a failure rate that high. At the end of the term, I walked away. What would I do now?

It would be over two decades before I found my passion.

I moved north to Seattle, Washington, worked an office job and filled the void by taking up ballroom dancing. Although this placed me in a crowd of "friends," I still struggled to build deep ties with anyone. The childhood lesson I learned as a minister's daughter—that they wouldn't like me if they really knew me—would not stay silent.

Then one day a tall, handsome Canadian stepped into my life offering what I had always craved and never expected to receive—unconditional love. A year later I found myself married and living in Vancouver, British Columbia.

Over the next fifteen years my life took a path I didn't expect. We were given very poor chances of having a family, but we beat the odds. Three beautiful children arrived so quickly we had trouble catching our breath—the oldest was only three and a half when the youngest was born. Daycare was way too expensive for three toddlers, so I became a stay-at-home mom.

I assumed I'd go back to work when the youngest entered grade one, but serious school bullying made that impossible. Several of the worst bullies were in after-school care, making that a dangerous option, and I felt safer taking my kids to and from school. On top of that, one of my children seemed to be struggling with a learning disability, but I couldn't get the school to take it seriously.

Someone needed to be there when the children came out of school to offer them a hug and a sounding board, to help pick up the pieces after a bad day. That someone was me.

Being a parent volunteer at school, joining the PTA, teaching occasional science classes for my youngest son's kindergarten class and volunteering to run school programs at the local nature park helped to keep my mind challenged.

The bullying my children faced at school made it difficult for them to build friendships among their classmates. Participating in outside activities provided a way to fill that void.

Driving three kids to their numerous activities meant having to spend a lot of time behind the wheel. The upside was this offered me a lot of wonderful one-on-one time with each of them. The downside was the fees required stretched our family budget to the limit.

To help with the finances I started sewing dance costumes from home—the most stressful thing I have ever done in my life. I had to accept as many orders as I thought I could handle without knowing exactly how many hours each would take. Deadlines were set in stone. If there was a delay of any kind—such as a problem finding the right fabric in the right color—the possibility arose that I would not finish in time. However, being late on a costume delivery was not an option as dancers taking the stage for a performance or a competition would be left with nothing to wear.

Fear was my constant companion. Day after day I was up at five in the morning working feverishly to meet my deadlines and there were many nights I didn't make it to bed at all. After five years I walked away and never looked back.

One day it was time to start figuring out what the next phase of my life would look like. My kids were all teenagers and needed me to take a serious step back. They were ready to stand on their own two feet and take personal control of their lives. That intensity I had as a child had been concentrated for so long on their needs; it now needed to be shifted in a new direction. It was time for me to find a new role.

I sat down at the computer and began to explore job opportunities on Craigslist. Almost immediately a New York fashion magazine ad for submissions caught my eye. Long-past high school dreams of writing novels bubbled up to the surface. Although those dreams had actually centered on me becoming a celebrated and well-known science fiction writer, I was willing to compromise and write about fashion.

My first thought was simply, "How hard can this be?" English had always been one of my best subjects in school. And who cared if I didn't know a single thing about fashion? I'd met a few local fashion designers I could interview through my daughter who had worked for them as a model. The rest I would just figure out along the way.

Fortunately when I hit reply I had no inkling that "hard" wouldn't even begin to describe the journey that lay ahead or I would never have had the courage. With great abandon and no true understanding of what I was getting into, I offered the magazine a few possibilities.

When the magazine accepted two of my story ideas, I handed the responsibility for the images over to an experienced photographer my daughter had worked with and set up a date to conduct the interviews. Next I purchased one of those little microcassette recorders for twenty-five dollars and a few extra mini tapes.

Full of excitement and totally oblivious to my lack of any training, off I headed for what I felt would be a fun afternoon doing something new and exciting. Instead, my entire life changed in a moment and a new career path opened up.

I have always been drawn to the stories of others, curious about every aspect of their journey and beliefs. What drives them? What circumstances have influenced them into becoming the person they are today? How have they come to embrace their current career?

In everyday life my curiosity had proved to be an unpopular trait. As an interviewer, this passion became an asset.

My first appointment was with designer and producer Denise Brillon. To this day, I am so grateful for Denise's kindness with my obvious inexperience. She shared deeply and openly. Her story gave me goosebumps many times. Two hours later I walked out the door full of excitement and ready to embrace a new career.

Everything about me comes together in interviewing. Those I interview offer me the gift of their journey—something I have always been driven to seek out—as well as some of the wisdom they have gained along the way.

In return, I offer them the gifts of listening as well as a

written article to promote their passion and to help the world get to know them a bit better. I like to call it "giving their story wings."

During interviews I also share from my life when appropriate—giving back some of the wisdom I hold in my pocket.

The first magazine ran out of money and folded before my articles reached publication. No one would hire me, so back I went back to Craigslist. Within a year of answering that first ad, and still with no experience to back me up, I became co-owner, editor, writer and more for a new online fashion magazine.

While our focus was on local talent, we quickly developed an international readership. Not long after I found myself writing on staff at another New York publication that featured both fashion and lifestyle articles, and publishing freelance articles in others.

Over the next decade my career as a writer involved a wild ride of laughter and tears—incredible highs and terrible lows. I alternately celebrated joyously and collapsed in despair.

There were many very dark moments after the magazine I co-owned dissolved. This was my baby. I had given four-and-a-half years of my life to building it. All my professional branding was connected with this magazine. It meant I had to completely start over and I honestly didn't know if I still had the energy.

There was also great joy when I finally realized my dream of becoming a published author. High or low, good or bad—each moment on this journey has brought me to this moment and I could not be more grateful.

I have had the privilege of interviewing over a hundred and fifty people in North America and around the globe. Each has touched my life in their own unique way. Each has freely shared their wisdom with me. One by one they have filled my pockets with pieces of gold and, whenever possible, I try to honor their gifts by passing their wisdom on to others.

Knowledge has also come through my own personal journey. And that, along with the wide variety of stories shared during my decade of interviewing, has helped me come to accept my own unique story.

I am exactly who I am meant to be. All the lumps and bumps that society wanted to sand off are actually my talents.

I came to understand more fully the beauty to be found in diversity. Diversity is humanity's greatest strength and is meant to be celebrated instead of feared. To do this, however, we must first learn to accept our own uniqueness. Only then can we fully extend that same gift to others and embrace them just as they are.

In the end this journey led me to discover my purpose, and when you discover your purpose the gloves come off. The universe has always been there waiting to guide you, but as you move toward your passion there are lessons to learn and skills to be gained. The road is not always easy, but each step along the way is essential even when the reason isn't clear.

What follows are just a few favorites out of the hundreds of pieces of wisdom that have been handed to me over the last decade, as well as a few that came to me as I walked my own unique path. I hope they will inspire you as much as they do me and that at least one will give you goosebumps. That's a sure sign you need to sit up and listen.

I don't know how to watercolor fade into the colors around me; I always feel like spilled ink, the accident on top of the purposeful paint below."
Tyler Knott Gregson, Poet, Author and Professional Photographer

~

Wabi-Sabi
The Beauty in Imperfection

During my early years of interviewing, I honestly had no idea how much I was being affected by what others shared. Without really recognizing what was happening, I began to listen and question the truth of my inner dialogue. I started to let go of my old, negative patterns of thought.

The first inkling of the inner changes that were occurring came during my time spent with photographer David Fierro.

Interviewing an artist is always inspiring. Artists have unique ways of looking at everything around them—seeing things in ways the rest of us often miss. If you're lucky, you might get at least a little glimpse of the world as they see it. David was more than willing to share his artistry and I was eager to experience it.

After interviewing him about his life journey from childhood to becoming the highly respected artist he is today, I turned to the subject of his inspiration. While this photographer embraces many different sources of inspiration, the one he described that brought me those telltale goosebumps was the Japanese concept of *wabi-sabi*.

There are many different ways of describing wabi-sabi, but the one I feel most drawn to comes from a book called *The Wabi-Sabi House: The Japanese Art of Imperfect Beauty* by Robyn Griggs Lawrence. This book is now definitely on my must-read list. Here are a few key points.

- Wabi-sabi is about embracing the beauty found in imperfection. A great example I've seen is a picture of a lovely ceramic bowl where a big crack in it has been filled with gold.

- Wabi-sabi encourages people to slow down and really experience their environment. Everything is constantly changing through nature's process of birth, then decay and finally death. We are an intricate part of this cycle. Stop, breathe, lean in close and see the minute details of the world that surrounds you.

- Wabi-sabi encourages finding joy and beauty in the signs of wear and tear that come with aging—wrinkles, thinning hair, worn clothing, faded colors, chipped dishes, dying foliage, paint peeling, weathered walls, rusting metal. Think of the changing color of fall leaves, an old piece of farm equipment rusting in a field or an amazing headshot of an aboriginal elder.

- Wabi-sabi also encourages us to find the beauty in what we see as our personal imperfections and this one can be a lot harder for some of us. For me I had to learn to embrace all the quirks that are an intricate part of my makeup.

The idea of wabi-sabi might have first hit like a bolt of lightning, but it was a slow process to fully integrate this principle into all areas of my daily life. As I began to embrace my quirks for what they add to my life, my focus turned from the situations where they are a negative to the many places they are an asset.

Slowly I began to move myself to a place of self-acceptance and self-love. With a sigh of relief, I let go of the idea that I need to fit into every social situation and that everyone should like me. Each unique facet reflecting my being is important. I began to embrace, celebrate and lovingly polish each one to shine brightly.

The biggest discovery I made during this time was that if we are critical of ourselves and do not love ourselves, we tend to surround ourselves with those who feel the same way. When I changed how I viewed myself, I suddenly began to draw a new group of friends who celebrate and accept my uniqueness the same way I do theirs.

Oh that I had discovered wabi-sabi in my twenties. Far too many years were spent brow beating myself for not being able to change and fit in, trying to become what society at large wanted me to be. What a waste of time.

"Just be yourself. Let people see the real, imperfect, flawed, quirky, weird, beautiful, magical person that you are."
Mandy Hale, Author, Speaker and Founder of The Single Woman Website

~

Ujamaa
Find Your Tribe

"U jamaa" was the next concept to really shift my viewpoint and the one that has had the biggest effect on how I live my life, both personally and professionally. This arose during my interview with Patti Desante—a former gas broker who walked away from a million-dollar paycheck to embrace the life of a Zen Buddhist Chaplain.

Ujamaa is a Swahili word meaning "familyhood." It formed the basis for social and economic development in Tanzania after the country gained independence from Britain in 1961, something I only learned recently. All I knew early on was that it became a guiding principle of Kwanzaa—a celebration that honors African heritage, first celebrated in 1966–67.

Patti had chosen the concept of ujamaa as the basis for a foundation she envisioned creating. The goal was to help disenfranchised populations create success in a way they felt meaningful—defined locally instead of by an outside organization. While wabi-sabi changed my internal view, ujamaa changed how I moved through the world around me.

Ujamaa embodies the idea of cooperative economics

or shared wealth. It puts forward the principle of coming together as a community—whether as a family, a village, a tribe, a group of close friends or a group with a common goal—to uplift all members as one, everyone equal with each other. The principle of ujamaa embraces the collective's sharing all resources as well as the obligation of all members to support, care and look out for each other.

When I talk about ujamaa, which I often do, the following is how I explain what this principle has come to embody for me personally and professionally: "We come together as a village to raise each other up."

Even in this moment, I get a physical reaction from sharing this personal definition. This is only my interpretation, but it resonates with me deeply and influences my life on a daily basis in a powerful way.

As the concept of ujamaa started to affect the way I viewed the world around me, I began to look more closely at who my friends were and who I did business with. Are we mutually supportive or are we in competition with each other? Do we have the same goals? Do we treat other people and businesses using the same moral compass?

First my inner circle of friends began to change. Slowly but surely, negative relationships started to fade away. No one is ever excluded from my life unless they choose to be emotionally or physically abusive, but my focus turned to nurturing those relationships that had a positive nature and are mutually beneficial.

I made the choice to set aside time to build these relationships through supporting and encouraging others in their passions. In return, they offered support and encouragement to me. We each took turns standing in the spotlight and sitting in the audience doing the cheering. No jealousy arose at the success of another. Instead we recognized that we each had our own unique journey to walk.

Next my business relationships changed. I became more selective, letting go of the idea that I have to embrace every opportunity, to work with everyone that enters the picture. I put every opportunity to work or collaborate to the same test.

Are we in competition or can we be mutually supportive? Do I have something to offer them in support of their goals? Do I have something to receive from them in support of my goals? If it is one-sided either way, I give the relationship a pass. I also turn a deaf ear to random criticism from those outside my ujamaa circle as it doesn't always come from a place of good intentions.

I do want to clarify one thing here. Being mentored is very different from establishing an ujamaa relationship. Mentoring is usually one-sided and given as a gift. I have had many mentors who have made a huge difference in my life. The way I pay their kindness back is first through gratitude and then through passing that same gift on by stepping into the role of mentor for another.

It is specifically in my personal and business relationships that I look for the principle of ujamaa to guide who I spend my time with.

"Call it a clan, call it a network, call it a tribe, call it a family. Whatever you call it, whoever you are, you need one."
Jane Howard, Author

"When you find people who not only tolerate your quirks but celebrate them with glad cries of 'Me too!' be sure to cherish them. Because those weirdos are your tribe"
A.J. Downey, Author

~

Get a Better Mirror

As a parent, it's always hard to watch your kids suffer. All three of my children were bullied through most of their school years. Seeing how much pain it caused them and how devastating it was to their self-confidence broke my heart. Thankfully over time they found their way to a place of self-acceptance, but there were many difficult times that will be hard to forget.

With this weighing heavily on my heart, it was no surprise to find myself crying buckets the first time I watched spoken word poet Shane L. Koyczan's YouTube video featuring his poem "To This Day: For the Bullied and Beautiful." If you haven't seen it yet, I can only say stop reading this and take a moment to check it out. Do it right now so you don't forget. I wasn't surprised that it quickly went viral and he was asked to perform it on the TedX stage. It's incredibly powerful.

Although the focus of this piece was to let those who have been bullied know they are not alone, there is a section that also talks about a person's journey to self-acceptance.

I can't tell you the number of times in dark moments of self-doubt I have re-read this passage in the transcript of his TedX Talk: "And if you can't see anything beautiful about yourself, get a better mirror. Look a little closer. Stare a little longer. Because there's something inside you that made you keep trying despite everyone who told you to quit.

These are words to live by.

So many times we allow what we see in ourselves to come from the outside world. That's okay if you've built your ujamaa tribe and let the reflection come from people who celebrate your uniqueness. Unfortunately, most of us let every single opinion around us, especially the negative ones, have an impact on how we view ourselves. It doesn't need to be that way.

When I first fell into co-owning a local online fashion magazine, I didn't care that I didn't have the right wardrobe, the industry knowledge or even a clue as to what I was doing. After being a stay-at-home mum for over fifteen years, I was excited just to be out in the world again facing new challenges and learning new skills. While there were a few who raised eyebrows at this inexperienced newcomer, my sheer joy and passion carried me through whatever arose.

Slowly things changed. The newness wore off and I became more aware I was usually the oldest woman in the room and definitely not the most fashionably dressed. The industry is focused on youth and I was middle-aged. Photographers were keener to take pictures of the young and hip; in fact, at one event I was asked to step out of the picture. Interviewers focused most often on rising talent and their images were the most likely to make it into any press covering the event. The hard truth that what you focus on becomes your reality is true.

With my enthusiasm waning, my lack of confidence began to rear its ugly head. My energy faded away and it became real work to be at events I used to enjoy. Sometimes I could hardly get out the door and when I did, I found myself walking into the event venue humbly instead of flying in full of enthusiasm. I became unsure of myself and didn't circulate to meet new people the way I used to.

A dear industry friend—Kris, someone who is also a part of my ujamaa circle—met me for coffee one day and helped me look at the issue. She mentioned she used to feel my energy when I came into a room and that that didn't seem to happen anymore. With love and concern she asked me what was going on.

Just having someone notice and then be incredibly supportive as I opened up and shared my internal struggles and growing doubt helped me move on.

We bury our insecurities, hiding them away and hoping no one will notice them. What I found that day was as soon as I gave my insecurities a voice and shone a light on the darkness, they lost their power. What I was experiencing was not built on fact. It was created out of fear.

This is when I realized how I saw myself was not how others saw me. That simple moment gave me permission to step back and look at myself through her eyes. And to be honest, the view was definitely better. What a difference.

Where I saw someone who didn't fit in, she saw someone who works hard, is passionate, has strong skills and has earned her place in the industry. She saw someone who is ready to promote and mentor others—an asset to her community.

It was a revelation.

Self-love is a life-long journey for me, but the universe is in charge and guides each step.

Reminders of this important bit of wisdom continue to reappear in my life at regular intervals from different sources. One day the excerpt I shared above from "To This Day" appeared in a poster on social media—a well-timed echo of what I had recently discovered.

A few years later I heard someone share an African saying that to the best of my memory goes something like, "You never really see yourself except through the eyes of another." Another well-timed echo.

Each time a new bit of wisdom comes my way I stop and take a moment to embrace the lesson it offers and consider how to use this knowledge to help me grow. I can never hear it enough.

Take a moment today to evaluate who you allow to influence your life. Choose the mirror you use to view your reflection wisely. As Shane says so poignantly in his poem, *"If you don't see anything beautiful it's time to get a different mirror."*

Kaleidoscopes and Diamonds

I love kaleidoscopes! It's inspiring to see those small colorful shapes come alive, forming constantly new and shifting images. My journey in self-doubt shared in the previous chapter is what led me to the concept of viewing each individual as though they are one of these popular kid's toys.

My lack of self-confidence wasn't just arising in social occasions; it affected how I looked at myself as a mother, writer, speaker and mentor. I would constantly browbeat myself for ways I could have handled things better. This needs no explanation for my role as a mother. Who hasn't had doubts at least once?

However as a writer, I would sit at the computer willing myself to type something, anything, onto that blank page while worrying nothing I wrote would be good enough. Nerves also took hold every time I took the stage to speak even though everything had usually gone fine in the past. Would I go blank? Would I be boring?

After my friend helped me to look at myself through her mirror and see the beauty of what I had to offer, I began to look at ways to change my internal view. In a quiet moment of introspection, the image that bubbled up from my core was of a kaleidoscope.

While it is a finite object put together in a simple way with a set number of little colorful pieces inside—it is also full of surprises. As you twist the chamber, each new view offered is just one unique picture from one of many wonderful combinations it is capable of offering. Perhaps I was the same.

Another wonderful analogy that arose offering me a different unique way of looking at myself was that of a multi-faceted diamond. What we see changes as light catches each different side. Whether kaleidoscope or diamond, my soul answered with a resounding YES!

In my life there are times I function as wife, mother, mentor, author, freelance writer, blogger and speaker. Each role I embrace is just one view, one facet, of what I offer the world. Each requires me to use a different skill set.

The solution to my self-doubt as I moved into the professional world was to let go of my mother/wife role and embrace my professional role. One needed to be set aside and another picked up. I had to twist the kaleidoscope to allow a new pattern to emerge or rotate the diamond to let the light showcase a different angle.

To get ready to go out to an event I learned to begin by considering why I had been invited. What will my role be this evening? Will I be there as media to cover the event? Or am I invited to promote and support the event by simply by being present? Have I been asked to speak this evening or to only be a part of the audience in support of another in my ujamaa tribe?

Once clear on my role, I would then review why they

chose to invite me specifically. What were my qualifications for being there?

By this time I had helped run a magazine for four years and been on staff at another in New York. I had written on events hundreds of times and knew what was expected. I had stepped up to speak on several occasions.

Once I fully embraced the knowledge that I came with the experience to be successful, the doubts began to fall away.

Next I dressed in a way that projected the image in line with the role I was fulfilling that evening. This wasn't for the benefit of those whom I met: it was to help me personally feel good about myself. Clothes do not have to be expensive or to stand out as unique. What they need to be is one more way to help you fully embrace who you are in that specific moment.

You need to choose what you wear as you walk each day of your life not by outside expectations, but by how your attire makes you feel. Close out the noise and let your wardrobe speak. Put your outfit on with confidence and add whatever hair and make-up makes you feel good. Go natural if that's the direction that feels best.

If I feel like being the center of attention at an event, I choose unique, striking or colorful clothing to set the tone. If I want to be understated, the direction I head when picking my garments focuses on subtlety.

Predictability isn't needed from one event to the next; you just need to listen to your heart. Your hair, makeup and clothing are only there in support of who you are in this moment in time. Make them ring true and you'll start to build confidence before you even walk out the door.

While I had to consciously embrace this process for several months, I have now internalized it and move through it without thinking. Who I am inside and the role I have the privilege of enjoying on any given night have become joined at the hip. In response, my confidence continues to rise.

> *"The sooner you step away from your smallness: the sooner you'll realize your greatness was waiting for you this whole time."*
> **Dena Patton, Igniting Greatness**

~

Your Quirks Are Your Talents

As I slowly began to embrace the concept of wabi-sabi, the way I looked at myself began to change.

I'm sure it was pretty obvious when you read my story in the first chapter of this book that because I did not fit into the box I was expected to, I assumed I was broken or that something was missing. Those two assumptions led me to embrace the idea that when I was formed, I was somehow not given a few key ingredients that others possessed.

I cannot even remember the number of times I heard, "Oh Marilyn! If only you could…" The implication was that if I changed, everyone would like me. I would be accepted. I would fit in. Life would be easier and happiness would flow.

All I needed to do was shave off what they considered to be my rough spots and fully step into the role my parents and society had laid out for me. If people didn't approve, then I needed to fix what was wrong with me.

For whatever reason, my nature just would not let me pretend to be someone I was not. My attitude was in your face—this is who I am, love me or don't. Let's get it out in the open now. Trusting another person enough to form a deep friendship was difficult.

Falling into a career of interviewing others is the second best thing that ever happened to me personally—my wonderful husband Glen and our incredible children, both birth and chosen, will always take first place. Every single interview opened a new door on a different journey. And as someone who will struggle eternally with Attention Deficit Disorder (ADD), I couldn't have chosen a better therapy than interviewing others and listening with my heart.

The people I interviewed shared freely about their own insecurities and how they moved beyond them (or were working through them) to embrace their passions. Each were living their life in their own unique way and—here comes the part that stunned me—without apology.

But it took time and many interviews under my belt before I noticed this truth.

One day it happened—the clouds parted, the sun began to shine and the angels began to sing. All the small bits of wisdom I had been receiving came together as one voice to offer me a new life lesson.

When looking back, I think the easiest way to explain a moment like this is an analogy—making soup. You have a pot into which you put ingredients, one after another. The burner is turned on. Then, after simmering for a while, all the individual elements blend into a new flavor experience that provides a beautiful and fulfilling meal.

For so many years I had accepted the outside world's truth that I was broken, that I needed to be adjusted and fixed. Suddenly I was given a different viewpoint that turned what I thought were negatives into positives worthy of being nurtured, embraced and cherished.

My racing mind, my intensity, my passion for others, my foot in my mouth, my lack of pretense and my total unconcern with social expectations were what made me unique. These traits weren't meant to be hidden or changed. Instead, I needed to plant them in the right garden and allow them to blossom.

Who I was at my very core was what made me excel at interviewing and was the reason people opened up so willingly. They could sense from my first question that I was fully present, incredibly interested and that there would be no judgment. They were safe sharing their lives with me.

What a relief! There was a purpose to it all!

A tremendous weight fell off my shoulders that day. It became easier to accept that there are situations in which I would never be fully comfortable. But now I knew the other side of the coin—I am who I am for a reason that is dear to my heart.

This isn't an excuse to be unkind or to not become the best person you can be. We each grow and change over our lifetime.

What embracing your quirks is all about is letting your uniqueness find a positive expression. When you find it, your passion and purpose will be there waiting.

"Remember, you are different than anyone else for a reason. A good reason. Find that reason and run with it."
Tay Jardine, Singer-Songwriter

Real People Living Real Lives

Look around you. Look at the factors influencing our children. What do you see? When I do this, I find myself truly disturbed.

We are raising a generation who are living their life glued to social media. Young people walk the streets and ride transit with their heads down, lost in their cell phones and tablets. Headphones blasting favorite tunes and podcasts keep everyone disconnected from those they are right next to.

Our role models seem to be chosen from whomever can promote themselves the best. Social media stars who have done little to earn their fame create mob scenes wherever they go. Success is defined through media images that tell us how we should look and what we should be accomplishing. If how we live, work, travel and dress doesn't measure up, then something must be wrong.

The 2016 election in the United States was the nail in the coffin for me. The whole process felt more like a reality television show than an intellectual process of selecting the best candidate. Whether you agree with the outcome or not, the whole debacle turned into what can best be described as a dirty street fight. Many chose to vote with their emotions and lines were drawn that will be hard to erase.

From a fairly young age, I was a real talker. I would strike up a conversation with anyone, whether a stranger or someone I knew, a habit I learned from my father. Many times I ended up monopolizing the discussion.

This habit was driven to even greater heights by my ADD. My friends and family members often raised their eyebrows as I talked non-stop, jumping from one subject to another, but I couldn't stop myself. Fortunately interviewing arrived to scratch this itch and I began to change.

Because it was obvious that I really did want to hear what these strangers had to share, people would tell me the most amazingly personal things. I treated each revelation with the respect it deserved. Each was a gift, stored in my memory with reverence.

What I came to realize over time was how important these everyday stories are. It's not just celebrities and successful business people who have wisdom to share; some of my more profound moments have happened during interviews with people who are not widely recognized.

It doesn't matter if their story is something that needs to be in a book shared with millions or simply told to family members. Every single person's individual journey is an intricate part of the fabric that makes up our generation— each piece one part of the total picture.

From the student just graduating design school, to the elevator technician next to me on the NYC subway, to the person in front of me at the bank—every single one of them has something to unique to offer. It can be a bit of wisdom, a life-changing moment or a funny behind-the-scenes story that makes me laugh. I never know what is coming. I simply open a new conversation without expectation.

From that realization on, I was disappointed each time I met someone truly private who chose not to share their journey. It meant there was a story I wouldn't get to hear and, if they never offered it to anyone, a story lost. I couldn't help but hope they would eventually find someone they were willing to share it with.

My mother was a prime example of this. We had a difficult relationship; she was very religious, I was not. Because of this, I never took the time in my younger years to listen to her share her personal journey. When I married and became a mother myself, however, things slowly began to change. We started to find common ground.

As our relationship began to grow, there were moments here and there when she opened up and shared some truly intriguing bits and pieces from her past. Not wanting to stop her flow of thoughts, I didn't make her wait while I grabbed my recorder. I chose instead to be fully present in that moment.

Each time she finished, I would encourage her to start making a recording or writing her stories down. I thought it would be a great project for her and couldn't wait to read what she wrote when it was finished. It never once occurred to me she wouldn't get around to it. She kept staying she would, "When she retired." But retirement never came.

At eighty-seven, my mother was still working part-time

in a private university. She awoke one Friday and as she started to get ready for work, she was hit with a massive stroke. Fortunately she had friends who checked up on her every morning and they rushed over as soon as they could not reach her by phone. Unfortunately the damage had already been done.

While she survived for two more weeks, she never was conscious enough to repeat those wonderful stories to me. It proved a double loss—my mother and her amazing life stories. I mourn the loss of both to this day.

Each time I get an urge to interview someone I think about this loss. It reminds me that I am part of a sacred trust that allows me to bear witness to the journey of another person and share it with the world.

If I can encourage each of you to do one thing, it's to get a recorder and take it with you every time you attend family events. Sit for a few minutes with your parents, grandparents, uncles and aunts. Turn on that recorder and stir their memory of times past. Let them reminisce without interruption. Or if you prefer, take a pad and paper, listen, and then find a quiet space after they finish to write it all down while the memories are fresh in your mind. Make a record of these stories while the person is still here to share them.

We allow ourselves to be inspired by what we see in the media or by those who take the stage to speak. We read self-help books looking for insight. We define the term "hero" by individuals who have faced incredible odds and survived.

I'm here to stand witness to the fact there is a broader definition of "hero." Sometimes the act of simply getting up every day and doing what needs to be done is heroic. The media never offers these stories, but they can be truly life-changing.

All you need to do is open the conversation and then just listen.

"Your time is your life. That is why the greatest gift you can give someone is your time."
Rick Warren, Author of The Purpose Driven Life

~

Journey Together

The bit of wisdom I call "journey together" presented itself time and time again through countless interviews, social media posts, articles and speakers. Because I feel this life principle is so important, and because of the sheer number of people who have shared it with me, you'll find the concept mentioned several times throughout this book. I hope the gentle echo will help bring home how important I feel it is to embrace the support of others.

If you only walk away with two things from this book, let them be the knowledge on how to build your ujamaa tribe and the wisdom that no one succeeds in a bubble. Whether you have one person or a hundred in your life, having support on your journey will have a huge effect on your ability to succeed.

Norwegian perfumer Geir Ness is one of the most positive people I know. When I first listened to him share his journey, I learned there never was a single moment when hearing the word "no" stopped him. It might have taken time, it might have taken hard work and the journey might have been difficult and long, but he always found a way to reach his dreams.

That just wasn't the way I had moved through life.

Self-doubt walked by my side and held me back for years. When I asked him what advice he had for people struggling with insecurity, his firm reply was to build a great team that supported your dreams and filled in the blanks where you were lacking.

In my interview with entrepreneur and luxury shoe designer Ruthie Davis, the same principle arose. I was honored to be allowed to include her story in my first book, but I struggled to get her chapter right. I was so impressed by her confidence and ability that I initially missed a key element—her gratitude for her amazing team. Over many conversations she also affirmed the truth that in business, no one succeeds alone, and went on to share that building a strong team was crucial to her success.

Embracing this concept meant letting go of many old connections and focusing instead on those with whom I could build mutually supportive personal and business relationships—my tribe. This is an ongoing process that continues to this day.

When writing my first book, I openly shared my highs and lows, my successes, my commitments and my struggles to put words to paper with this circle. They offered support freely. They always had my back.

One day while suffering a serious case of writer's block, all I needed to get the ball rolling was having another industry friend, Nicolette, ask me at an event how it was going. When I shared my struggle, she urged me to go home and get to work. She followed that up with a Facebook comment giving me a gentle push to make progress on my book. Because of her encouragement I ended up writing half a chapter that day. I wonder if she even remembers the incident.

In fact any time someone cared enough to ask how the book was coming along, I could feel my confidence rise.

There was a crucial moment when I decided I couldn't possibly succeed and was going to quit writing completely— no more articles, no more blogs and not a single book in my future. I paused with my finger poised over the delete button for quite a while. In the end, what stopped me was simply the support I had received. I wanted to prove that everyone's belief in me was justified.

One memory that stands out came after I finalized my first book and sent it to the printers. For better or worse the manuscript was complete. At that moment all I felt was tremendous relief and I shared the moment on my Facebook page. It was then that a long-time industry friend, Garry, whom I had met before my writing journey began commented, "I always knew you could do it. I never had a single doubt." I was stunned. How could he know what I didn't know myself?

I wish I could mention the name of every person who has given me an encouraging word or a push to get moving again. Unfortunately there are just too many—a village full.

A heartfelt thanks to all of you; you know who you are. You have had my back each step along the way and I couldn't be more grateful for your support.

"Ubuntu—I am what I am because of who we all are."
A Nguni Bantu Saying

"If you want to go fast, go alone. If you want to go far,
GO TOGETHER."
An African Proverb

"People either inspire you to greatness or pull you
down in the gutter, it's that simple. No one fails alone,
and no one succeeds alone."
Eric Thomas, Motivational Speaker and Author

Pieces of Gold

When artist Pamela Masik mentioned "pieces of gold" in our first interview, I was so struck by the concept that I became lost in thought for the next few minutes and didn't hear what followed. Thankfully I record all interviews so I didn't miss anything and as my mind races ahead, it didn't take me long to catch up.

I'd like to share an excerpt from my first book about that moment.

"Choosing to put herself out as an artist challenged that negative inner voice, but it was an important step in healing. 'I had to learn self-love. I would stand there with my hand trembling trying to paint—worried that the next brush stroke would mess up the whole thing. I had to overcome that fear....' One day during a moment of clarity, an earth-shaking realization set in—she suddenly understood how art can heal. 'I had a little piece of "gold" in my pocket that would also help other people.'" (quoting Pamela Masik in *Life Outside the Box*).

The phrase "pieces of gold" comes to mind often now, especially when I am privileged to share the wisdom I hold with others. Hearing it that day also provided me with the initial inspiration to write *The Wisdom of Listening*.

The image of gold carried in everyone's pocket was quickly integrated into how I looked at others. There are times in interviews when I physically react to a comment or story—usually through goosebumps or a heightened awareness, like someone just tapped me on the shoulder. I always sit up and pay attention when this happens as it means I have just been offered something really important. It is a gift I need to recognize, accept and share.

When my friend Steely Springham opened her talk at PowHERhouse Vancouver with, "Do you see what I see?" I sat up in my seat. It was like being zapped. Her opening words had a message for me far beyond what she envisioned when she conceived her topic for that day. The image that instantly sprang to mind was being on stage and looking at a room full of people, pockets overflowing with wisdom just waiting to be shared.

I now carry the image of people with their pockets bursting everywhere I go. No matter what event I am at, each roomful of people is another opportunity to perhaps receive a new bit of wisdom and to possibly share one of mine with another.

We normally look to speakers, leaders and life coaches for help and guidance, but in truth it could be the person setting next to you on the bus. Every day, every single person you meet holds wisdom gleaned from their unique life. You never know who will have the nugget you have been seeking.

Where this gets tricky is the process of learning when it's your turn to give and when it's your turn to receive. With my racing mind, I'm always ready to jump in when an idea pops into my head. Learning to be silent has been more difficult. I still have a long way to go.

There is no single answer on how best to fine-tune your internal radar in this area. It's a slow process of learning how to be silent and listen for those gentle nudges. If you want to practice, try entering a room and pausing for a while in a quiet corner. Let your eyes take it all in. It doesn't have to be an event, just a place with people in it.

Where are your eyes drawn to? Whose face looks interesting?

Listen to that inner voice and then have courage. Walk over and open a conversation and see where it leads. You'll never know until you open the door.

"We cannot understand each other until we truly learn to listen."
Nina Shoroplova [from *Trust the Mystery*], Author and Book Editor

"Gaining knowledge, is the first step to wisdom. Sharing it is the first step to humanity."
Unknown

Everyone Starts Somewhere

Around the time the excitement of being back out in the world was ebbing and the reality of my inexperience as a fashion writer was hitting home, I landed an interview with designer RozeMerie Cuevas of JAC (formerly Jacqueline Conoir). From the moment I walked into her large, combined retail and work space filled with beautiful high-end garments, I knew I was out of my league.

RozeMerie had set aside time in her busy schedule for this interview. In return I had promised to do a feature article in my magazine. This was a time I needed to dig deep and find some confidence as it would be unprofessional to cancel at the last moment. Inside, though, all I wanted to do was flee before she arrived.

I still remember looking down at my discount-shoe-rack footwear and low-end bargain clothing with shame. To save money, my husband had given me my last haircut. My eye wear was obviously from a cheap outlet and I don't know if I even had makeup on. Were my fingernails at least clipped? I couldn't remember. What did I think I was doing?

Fortunately, RozeMerie walked in before I totally lost it and offered a lovely, welcoming smile. Her eyes never moved to take in my attire. She focused on my face and gave me her full attention.

Still nervous, my saving grace was that I start all my interviews with the same four opening questions. "Where you born? Where did you grow up? What were you like as a child, as a teen? Looking back, can you remember any moments that hinted you would embrace this career?"

Having this set opening gave me a few moments to catch my breath and get my feet back under me.

The nugget she had to share with me came early on. It was a story I've heard her tell many times since, and I still love it to this day. But in that moment it was fresh and new—and it was just what I needed to hear. I will always be grateful.

When RozeMerie was in her teens, her family tried to guide her toward professional studies that offered a safe and bright financial future. She initially embraced that path while doing some sewing in her spare time as a hobby. She loved making her own design ideas come to life. Friends noticed and were impressed by the garments she created. Soon she found herself sewing for them as well.

One day a friend mentioned there was a small fashion show being run in a local nightclub and urged her to consider taking part. Scary as it was, the idea would not go away. With no real knowledge of what to expect, RozeMerie decided to jump in and give it a try—just like I did with writing.

The day of the show arrived. This young designer showed up at the venue with her garments packed in trash bags only to see everyone else with theirs inside garment bags which were carefully hung on rolling racks. They looked so professional and composed.

Nerves quickly took hold. What did she think she was doing? It was a feeling I could relate to all too well. As she continued the story I was drawn into her tale, totally mesmerized.

After the show RozeMerie found herself in the bathroom hugging the toilet, overcome by nerves. Hidden away in her stall, she heard two women walk in and start discussing the different collections. One they complimented in particular was hers. In that moment her future shifted completely. She knew she would be a fashion designer.

I no longer know if I heard the phrase "everyone starts somewhere" in one of RozeMerie's talks or if it bubbled up from within after hearing her story. Either way, it was the gift she offered me that day.

Listening to her early fears and inexperience helped me realize it was okay that I was new to the game and still learning the ropes. It didn't matter that I didn't have a wardrobe full of amazing clothes yet or hundreds of interviews behind me. We each start somewhere. This was my beginning.

I can't thank RozeMerie enough for sharing this memory with me that day. The wisdom she offered has had long-lasting effects during my journey, especially every time I embrace moving in new directions. I am also honored that she has continued to be a supporter and mentor throughout my career.

Many of her designs have become cherished garments in my wardrobe and I am sure I will add new ones in the future. They are part of my regalia.

"The expert in anything was once a beginner."
Helen Hayes, Actress

~

Never Too Late

In my early adult years, I honestly never thought aging would bother me in the least. Looking back at my young twenty-to-thirty-something self, I can only laugh at how naive I was. A common phrase comes to mind: ignorance is bliss.

Along with my rising number of years on this planet have come a lot of unexpected situations. I went through menopause at the early end of the spectrum, long before anyone else I knew did. That meant I had no one to get advice from or to commiserate with.

No worries. I danced with joy at this milestone and celebrated that the transition was annoying but not difficult to handle. Life was good.

Then came a few surprises. There were unwelcome changes to my body—a new roll around the middle and a few annoying chin hairs that needed constant plucking. Several injuries that had healed long ago came back to haunt me. Some people began to roll their eyes as I shared my opinions, and one person even said, "You have to forgive Marilyn. She's older. She doesn't understand." Whoa!

As I've mentioned before, it was becoming increasingly clear to me that the images captured at fashion events were largely focused on the young adult crowd, unless you were one of those rare exceptions held up in the media—think Jennifer Lopez or Christie Brinkley.

Upon discovering my age, people began telling me how great I looked and that "age is just a number." Those last words began to annoy me like fingernails scraped across a chalkboard.

Men and women I knew began to lose their jobs in their mid-fifties and were replaced with younger employees who were often offered far less pay. As these mature men and women searched for new positions, they found the market for age and experience had undeniably and significantly slimmed. Everyone I saw in the media, other than industry icons, was becoming younger and younger while I found myself moving without fail in the other direction.

When my kids were grown and I tried to move back into the workforce, I had to start at the very bottom. The jobs that opened up had heavy workloads, tons of pressure and incredibly low wages. Thankfully, I had already begun to embrace interviewing and writing. It wasn't long before I turned my focus on both full time.

When I was a young mom, I heard those looking at the future say our children would need to be ready to refocus and change careers at least four times over their lifetime. Forget the next generation: it became something I did myself. I moved from studying psychology to working in an office, to being a stay-at-home mum, to volunteering, to sewing dance costumes, to working in an office again, to writing and running a magazine, to becoming a published author. Perhaps that puts me ahead of my time.

Starting a new career at a later age was a joyful thing for me, but the world didn't readily open its arms and say, "Thank goodness you're finally here! We've been waiting for you!" I had to get creative.

I was fifty when I answered that Craigslist ad for magazine submissions. They actually offered me a good financial compensation, something I subsequently learned was rare in today's tough market. However, my articles were to be published in the third edition and the company folded while that issue was at the printers. They had run out of money.

Not only did I not get paid, I didn't get published. I alone was responsible for telling the photographic team it had fallen apart. They were more experienced than I was so took it better than I did.

Despite this setback I was undeterred. This new passion would not be denied—its siren call kept me awake at night. The question now became how to find a new door to open. I reached out in many ways to established media sources, but the only response was the discouraging sound of crickets chirping.

Here I was, an older woman—now fifty-one—with no degree in journalism and no published work to her credit. Between my age and my lack of a resume, why would a media source give me a chance? There was a large pool of young talent lying in wait with a lot more experience to offer.

After hitting dead ends for six months, I went back to Craigslist and posted something along the lines of, "Writer with some connections in the local fashion industry looking for an opportunity to practice. No compensation required."

Looking back, I probably would let go of that last sentence, even though it was true at the time. But the ad brought results. It connected me with a photographer who wanted to start a magazine highlighting talent in our local fashion community.

This single ad opened the door to co-owning, editing and running a magazine for four and a half years. It brought me the opportunity to work on staff with another magazine in New York and be published in a third in London.

I dropped a pebble in a pond and it ended up creating a tsunami that furthered my career and eventually led me to becoming a published author.

When the person I co-owned the local magazine with and I decided to dissolve our partnership and fold our publication, I realized it was time to reevaluate my focus on shorter articles. I had become increasingly frustrated that the allowable word count for magazine submission was so low. The stories I shared had so much more depth available. Tons of great material was being left unused on the cutting room floor. Financial compensation, even when offered, rarely came through.

On a whim, I attended a talk by Julie Salisbury, founder of Influence Publishing and InspireABook. From the moment she began speaking, I had that telltale physical reaction of goosebumps along with a new one, a few tears. The impact was so strong I couldn't even focus on what she was saying. I knew without a doubt I had found a new mentor who would help me on the road to becoming an author.

True to form, I made a leap of faith and dove into deep water without a thought to what might lie ahead. I attended an InspireABook mastermind weekend workshop where I laid out the title, subtitle, chapter titles, chapter outlines and back cover for my book. After it was over, I was offered a publishing contract and immediately signed on the dotted line.

Contract in place, it was time to begin writing. I thought that having over five years of experience behind me meant this obviously would be an easy and joyful process. I also thought that writing the longer chapters needed in a book wouldn't be a problem as I had always struggled to stay within the required low word count for magazine articles. I was mistaken.

Self-doubt reared its head as I began chapter one. I stalled out at two thousand words, thirty-two hundred words short of my book-chapter goal. I needed additional material and more practice writing longer pieces.

What should have been a six-month journey stretched into eighteen months of starting, stopping, insecurity and worry. This was not how I expected it to unfold.

I reached the finish line with the support of Julie, my publishing team and my supportive circle of friends. When I took the stage at my book celebration—not a launch, a celebration with my community—only five days after turning sixty, it was with a tremendous sense of satisfaction and a deep well of gratitude.

Do I wish the journey had been more joyful? Yes. Do I wish I had found this career earlier? Absolutely. However, I believe everything comes to us at the perfect and right time, that the experience is what it is meant to be. Each and every moment is an important step in learning that brings us ever closer to perfection.

I took a new direction at fifty. Began a new career at fifty-one. Launched my first book at sixty. I am a prime example that it is truly never too late to embrace your passion, to learn something new or to dive into unknown waters.

We are meant to continue learning throughout our entire life. We are meant to face challenges. It's what keeps us young inside and makes life exciting. Whether for pay or pleasure, commit to learning one new thing every year for the rest of your life.

There is one author, now deceased, who comes to mind every time I find myself worrying about my age and whether I have more to accomplish. His story has had such a huge impact on my life that I would like to close this chapter by sharing it with you.

Harry Bernstein was born in 1910 and wrote magazine articles, read scripts for various movie production companies and worked as a magazine editor for trade magazines. In his spare time, he pursued his dream of writing books. Over the years he wrote forty of them, but each and every one was rejected. He gave up, destroyed most of the books and focused on his "real" work.

In 2002, his wife of sixty-seven years passed away. Bernstein was devastated. To fill the empty void, he sat down at the typewriter and began to write the story of his early years in poverty, his abusive father and his mother's struggles to keep the family going. He titled it, *The Invisible Wall: A Love Story That Broke Barriers*. He was ninety-three.

He sent his finished manuscript off to the London office of Random House where it languished for a year before being noticed by editor Kate Elton, who described it as "unputdownable." The rest is history.

The Invisible Wall hit bookstores in 2007, and Bernstein followed it up with *The Dream* in 2008 and *The Golden Willow* in 2009. At the age of ninety-eight, Bernstein was awarded a Guggenheim Fellowship to further pursue his writing. Before passing away at the age of a hundred and one, Bernstein declared his nineties the most productive years of his life. It truly never is too late.

"It's never too late to become what you always wanted to be in the first place."
J. Michael Straczynski, Screenwriter, Producer and Director

Not My Job

Growing up as a minister's daughter left me with a very clear message—the only life worth living is a life of service. Other people are what matter most. You should put everyone's needs in front of your own and always think about yourself last. To do otherwise was unforgivably selfish.

This was also the societal message I received about my roles as a wife and a mother. My needs should come last. If I did it right, everything would turn out fine and everyone would be happy. Thinking back on how I held onto these beliefs for so long I can only shudder. The weight of responsibility and the guilt from failure was overwhelming.

Every single person who came into my life mattered to me. I wanted them each to live a good life and enjoy the best of health. I wished for them to have food on the table, a roof over their heads, a passion to drive them and friends to support them.

If anyone told me they were suffering for any reason, my maternal instincts would turn on high. I needed to help them. It was my responsibility to find a solution and get them back to a good place. If I truly cared, I should be able to make their lives better.

The emotional weight was tremendous and the way I chose to "help" not always welcome.

In recent years, the knowledge that we need to take care of ourselves first and foremost has been gaining recognition. When we are in a healthy space personally we have more to give. When we take care of our mind and body it allows us to offer our very best to others. What a relief.

However, I couldn't shake that original message totally. Somehow that early admonishment to put others first just wouldn't go away. Slowly the emotional burden I put on my shoulders began to bleed over into the rest of my life. Sleep and focus on my own journey would be lost as I struggled to find a solution for others.

One amazing mentor in my life is Sue Dumais, the founder of Heart Led Living. Simply hearing her voice affects me in a positive way. I've listened to her speak on stage several times and am always left with a new insight.

Sue connects members of her Heart Led Living group through a weekly phone session. Those participating can just listen, ask for guidance or share personal experiences. In a time of serious struggle I also reached out to her privately for a one-on-one session to explore what was going on.

One week I was feeling particularly overwhelmed by the struggles of several people I knew. The problems they faced had no easy answers—mysterious and debilitating physical problems that doctors couldn't seem to figure out, difficult business situations and unwelcome financial challenges.

My question to Sue was, "How do we care deeply for others without getting bogged down emotionally?"

Her reply was a simple but profound question: "Is it your job?"

For a moment I was speechless. Those four words changed everything. I realized my early training that I should "always" put everyone else's needs before my own was utterly and completely wrong.

The discussion that followed provided the impetus for another big shift in how I looked at the world around me. I hope I can find the right words to share my personal insight with you as it can be hard to explain.

We are surrounded by people who need support in a myriad of ways. Most of us do not have the financial ability, unlimited time or emotional capacity to help absolutely everyone. It can be discouraging to find ourselves in a place of privilege and peace and know we do not have the resources to help those we know who are not in the same place.

Guilt can also play a huge role. Why is my life so good when theirs is so hard? Responses can range from walking away feeling the situation is hopeless, to jumping in too aggressively with only our personal idea of what the solution is to guide us. A raging bull in a china shop does more harm than good.

When these situations arise, it's time to step back and consider if we are being led to action. Our intuition—our inner voice—is always waiting to guide us. Our mind tends to go down expected paths, but our intuition looks at our journey more creatively.

What Sue shared with me that day was that if I was meant

to step in and help, my intuition would show me the way. It would be a clear path. If I was struggling and floundering with no concept of what to do, then in that moment it wasn't my job. I needed to step back, let go and trust.

You cannot imagine how freeing this was for me, but it does take constant practice to not fall back into old patterns.

I still care deeply and always hold a safe space for every person who reaches out to me. I give them my time and my attention. I listen with my full being. I am ready and willing to hear their struggles and stand behind them emotionally. I hold them close and let them know they are cherished.

Each time a difficult conversation ends, I try to find a place of stillness to just listen to my inner voice. Is it guiding me in any direction? Is there something I need to be doing?

If I am led to act, I follow through. If not, I know that my role is to continue to support and hold space for them. I also need to step aside to make space for the answer or help that is already coming their way.

The guilt is now gone and, with that, the weight I was carrying. It's always a privilege to have someone reach out to me for support. Now that I have let go of the guilt, I can give them the best of myself fully and freely.

"No one can do everything, but everyone can do something."
Max Lucado, Author

~

Embrace the Feeling—
Let Go of the Story

I spoke about meeting Zen Buddhist Chaplain Patti Desante in my chapter on ujamaa. However, that is only one of the many truths she's shared with me over our long friendship. I am excited to offer another of Patti's gems that has had a huge effect on my life: embrace the feeling and let go of the story.

After our first interview, Patti and I connected through social media and over coffee many times. I was privileged to share her story in the New York magazine I worked for and to support one of her amazing trips to Malawi.

We reached out to each other during high and low moments, always knowing we'd receive what we needed most—someone to hold space for us with warmth and understanding. Every once in a while there would also be a helpful idea shared.

While my kids were growing up, I spent time volunteering in their elementary school. It was through talking with their teachers, I realized my racing mind and my intensity were strong indicators of ADD. I needed to know more and quickly began to read numerous articles on the subject. As I researched the possibility, so much began to fall into place.

At first I considered ADD to be a defect. Then, as I learned to accept the fact that I am exactly who I am meant to be, I came to realize what a gift ADD is. That said, even the most wonderful of gifts can come with a challenge or two.

I find it hard to slow my racing mind when it starts zooming down a path. This is usually okay during the day, but it can keep me awake for hours if it happens in the middle of the night. Sometimes I have to get up for a while and let it run its course.

I couldn't help laughing the other day when another person with the same struggles described it as, "The squirrels are out!" So true.

My intensity also has its upsides and its downsides. It is a complete and welcome asset when I'm pursuing my passion. But when something negative happens, that laser focus can hone in, clasp on tight and have me gnawing on it for days. This is especially true of situations where someone has chosen to cause me emotional pain.

Whenever this occurred in the past I just couldn't let it go. The incident and the hurt would bounce around inside me for days or weeks causing negative emotions, distress, difficulty sleeping and great heartache. I tried meditation, affirmations, exercise and distraction to no avail.

One day I shared this problem with Patti and in response, she handed me this wonderful piece of gold, *"Embrace the feeling—let go of the story ."* I still remember the exact moment Patti shared it with me. It was the answer I had been waiting for and my heart resonated with this wisdom.

What Patti explained to me was that all emotions are true and they are meant to be expressed. Weep, let the tears run, pound or scream into your pillow, rant and rave, laugh until you cry, hug with joy.

There were two pieces of advice that came along with this truth. Be sure to choose a safe environment to express your emotions, especially negative ones. And before you let difficult emotions run free, you need to first let go of the story—the why. It is the story that binds those negative feelings to you.

Letting go of the why behind the hurt is not always easy. We are raised as social creatures and prefer situations where we are liked. Unfortunately, everyone receives criticism at some point. Remember, the only influence someone else has on your life is what you allow them to have. Their words are not your truth.

Instead of holding on to negative experiences, you can choose to release them. Any time the memories try to bubble up you simply and consciously release them again.

With this advice in mind, I began a slow and steady journey of putting what I had learned into practice. Each and every time a hurtful situation arose, I purposely took time to recognize this story was not mine and visualized it floating away. Then I gave myself permission to allow the feelings of sadness and hurt to bubble up from deep within.

By allowing myself to experience these emotions without getting caught up in the reason behind them, I found that the feelings would wash through me by the end of the day.

It took time, but slowly the constant practice began to produce amazing results. No matter what difficult issues arose, I could sleep without tossing all night. And I could wake up the next morning fresh and ready to face a new day.

As with all things you practice, the process slowly becomes internalized. Over time I find myself affected less and less by any hurtful actions in the first place. Now it's the rare moment when I need to remind myself to let go of the story. The process has become almost second nature.

"Give yourself permission to feel anger, pain, resentment. Relax, then let it go with love."
Unknown

~

A Change Conundrum

A poster holding the following quote by Dean Jackson, marketer and author, inspired this chapter: "When she transformed into a butterfly, the caterpillars spoke not of her beauty, but of her weirdness. They wanted her to change back into what she always had been. But she had wings."

As with so many truths included in this book, once the idea presented itself to me it wouldn't go away. "Change" would drift through my mind as I dropped off to sleep at night and be the first thing to grab my attention upon waking.

One morning I decided I need to explore what my heart was trying to tell me. I stayed in bed a little longer and allowed my freshly awakened mind the freedom to explore this quote from a deeper perspective. Why did what it shared about change affect me so deeply? What was I meant to share with you?

It all begins with my journey as a writer.

After I answered that first Craigslist ad and shared with my family that I'd had two articles accepted, my kids smiled. They were happy I had shifted my laser focus away from them and in a new direction.

My husband Glen was not as excited. He had watched me struggle as a stay-at-home mum trying to deal with the reality of bullying, and then as I worked on the side as a dance costumer always buried under the stress of deadlines. Out of love, he wanted me to find a new direction where stress would not rear its ugly head. He wanted to come home to a happy, calm partner living a life that gave her joy.

Interviewing changed my life. Everyone in my social circle could tell I was passionate about this new career and, for the most part, my family was initially supportive.

I also had a friend, Norma, who was totally excited for me. Fortunately she is also great at English, so she offered to edit my early work. I still smile when I remember her saying, "'Got' is such a common word. Can you replace it with something better?" She was right.

As I moved into co-owning a magazine, the pressure began to build. The responsibilities were enormous. My business partnership was, as to be expected, rocky at times and self-doubt added to my overall stress. This was not what Glen had hoped for. My suffering broke his heart.

What no one—including myself—understood at the time was that I was on a life-changing journey. If I could take my current self back and do it all over again, the road would have been much easier. But it was the trials of walking this path that would bring me through many difficult times to the knowledge I have now gained. My pockets are overflowing with pieces of gold.

I remember one particularly bad time. Totally frustrated,

I was talking with my husband about this or that problem and laying out all the difficulties, searching for sympathy. He looked at me and said just one word, "Quit."

What followed was a discussion of the fact that writing wasn't bringing in any money, so obviously it was only a hobby. Dealing with the heavy pressure I was under wasn't worth it.

It was in that moment I realized almost everyone close to me, Norma excepted, thought this was a hobby I was exploring to keep myself busy. They didn't understand the passion that drove me, and they definitely did not understand why I could not walk away. Truth be told, I'm not sure I fully understood it either.

Suddenly I felt completely and utterly alone.

At the same time the message was clear. I needed to quit complaining and instead start finding solutions. The answer when it came was not the one I wanted. It was time to fold the magazine and move on. The loss I felt as I embraced this truth was deep.

Little did I realize the universe was clearing my slate as a new and exciting adventure was in store—writing my first book. Thank goodness there are times we don't have any control over what is happening. Look what we would miss!

Again, this was initially perceived as just a new direction for my "hobby." I have no idea if anyone in my family thought I would ever finish; even I seriously doubted my success. The journey stretched out far longer than expected as I struggled with self-doubt. But with the support of my growing group of amazing friends, I reached the finish line.

That was when a really wonderful moment happened.

Three days before my party to celebrate the launch of my book, my husband walked into the living room and from the bottom of his heart expressed how very proud he was of me for realizing this dream. The tears flowed. It was all I ever wanted.

Rather than organizing a book signing, I chose to have a party to commemorate this amazing milestone. My entertainment at the launch included an African drummer and dancer, a Tahitian dancer, two amazing singers, a wonderful burlesque performer and a drag queen who also emceed the evening.

Over a hundred and fifty people came to celebrate with me. In honor of turning sixty a few days before, I handed out cupcakes.

At the end of the evening I was on a huge adrenalin high. This evening was everything I could have dreamed of and more. It was a night to remember, and to this day I am filled with gratitude for all the support I received.

After the event I heard my husband talking on the phone. He was proud of my accomplishment and astounded by the fact so many had attended and purchased books. I basked in the afterglow, but a few months later that glow ended.

I thought I would head into writing book two soon after launching the first. I was full of enthusiasm and had big plans to write at least five more books. Instead, the demands of learning the ins and outs of marketing filled my hours. Incredible self-doubt again reared its ugly head.

When I shared this with Glen, his response was, "Haven't you reached your goal? Aren't you done?"

I was stunned. I share some of the responsibility for this because I hadn't talked much about my long-term goals due to being so consumed with doubt. Still, it surprised me.

What I learned through this process was that whatever was happening inside of me was personal. No one can know or fully understand another's journey. As long as people have our backs, we can't ask for more. Every one of our friends, family and supporters are doing the best they can to help us while only having access to what they see going on from the outside. They have no idea what our inner dialog might be.

Never let your validation come from another person. No matter how loving the advice is or who it comes from, those around you may find themselves fearful for you or confused by your growth. You are changing in front of their eyes while they might not be. And that's okay. Embrace whatever positivity they have to offer and let the fears they express fall away.

You are meant to change. You are meant to transform into a butterfly. No one can hold you back except you.

"It takes a lot of courage to release the familiar and seemingly secure, to embrace the new. But there is no real security in what is no longer meaningful. There is more security in the adventurous and exciting, for in movement there is life, and in change there is power."
Alan Cohen, Author

~

There Is No Secret

I first met Canadian tap icon and talented dance choreographer William Orlowski at a three-day workshop my daughter took as a teenager. I danced all through my twenties, so I couldn't resist peeking in just a bit to watch. It quickly became clear that what he offered was unique.

Classically trained, this teacher's tap technique was totally different than the loud stomping style that had become popular in recent years. With a tiny flick of his ankle, a quiet but distinct sound could be heard all the way to the back of an auditorium. I watched in awe, having never seen anyone tap like this.

When William came out in the hall for a break after class, my curiosity won out. I had to go up and talk with him. I was instantly put at ease by his warm and approachable manner and quickly came to feel as though we had known each other for a long time.

In that first conversation, I learned he had just been diagnosed with Parkinson's; my oldest brother had recently received the same diagnosis. This revelation opened the door to a much deeper discussion on the challenges both were facing. The seeds of friendship were planted that day.

The condition was putting limits on William's work as a

choreographer and dancer, but surprisingly that didn't seem to dampen his vision for what he intended to accomplish. William radiated positive energy and he had a seemingly endless list of things he planned to do. It was a joy just to stand close and soak it all up. This was before I began my career as a writer, so I walked away not expecting to ever see him again.

A few years later I connected with him again and learned that what doctors had originally thought was Parkinson's had turned out to actually be an aggressive form of dystonia—a debilitating neurological movement disorder that features painful and repetitive contractions, spasms and abnormal body positions. William ended up confined to a bed, contorted with spasms. It seemed like a cruel fate for an artist whose life embraced movement.

Then science stepped in with a miracle. He was approved for Deep Brain Stimulation (DBS) surgery, something normally associated with treatment for Parkinson's. The procedure is only available to patients whose symptoms cannot be controlled by regular medications. A battery-operated neurostimulator about the size of a stopwatch is implanted in the brain to deliver electrical stimulation to the areas responsible for movement and to block the abnormal nerve signals responsible for a patient's tremors and spasms.

Once the operation was over and William was back in recovery, he decided he had to go to the bathroom. Without thinking he got out of bed, rising and standing with little effort, and started to walk. His sister had to stop him and get him to take notice of this incredible moment. It hadn't happened in a while. He also gained back three inches in height that the spasms had taken from him.

Almost immediately, William was back at work teaching, mentoring, creating new choreography and occasionally performing. At this point I had begun pursuing my writing career and I was desperate to interview him for an article. However, I quickly hit a snag. Most of the publications I worked with—fashion and lifestyle magazines—were not interested in an article on a dancer.

Finally I connected with a Canadian dance magazine. Although they would only give me a small sidebar, it was all the excuse I needed to do a full interview. Unfortunately, by this time William lived in Toronto and had no plans to travel back to Vancouver anytime soon. In fact I never saw him in person again.

I ended up interviewing him twice, both times from a distance. For the dance article we made do with a Skype interview, a medium that I find doesn't always let a person's personality come through. He had the gift of storytelling, though, and managed to draw me in.

When the chance arose to write about him again for inclusion in my first book, we connected through the phone. Our conversation brought me up to date on what had occurred since our last interview, as well as how he dealt with the new limitations that arose as his disorder continued to progress.

I asked how he kept a positive attitude even in the face of adversity. I asked how he coped with only being able to work half days instead of full days as a choreographer—something that held him back from many opportunities. I asked him what advice he had for young people just starting out. I asked him for his definition of success.

It didn't matter what I asked, he had one firm reply, *"There is no secret, just do and be brave."* Each time we spoke William shared those same nine words of wisdom with me. Over time they have become one of my personal mantras.

How much simpler could life be? Get up each morning, be brave and dive into whatever adventures lie in wait. This is exactly how William chose to face the difficulties life threw at him. The reality that his time was limited didn't hold him back; it drove him to work even harder.

As his dystonia progressed, he endured three more brain surgeries to install new DBS devices to deal with his increasing limitations. Through it all he composed new choreography, taught blind children to tap, created new works for a group that took theater to seniors and painted Japanese watercolors.

There was one conversation in which William surprised me by sharing a regret. His focus was always extremely positive and he rarely would let a negative word escape his lips. His one regret was that he knew he would never live long enough to accomplish everything on his list.

To be honest, even if he had been given a long, healthy time on earth, I'm not sure he ever would have finished. There was no end to the creative pursuits he wanted to explore or the passions that called to him.

I lost my wonderful friend and mentor in October 2016, but I still feel his influence daily. When fear sets in, when writer's block threatens, when I feel time is too short or that I'm in over my head, I remember his words.

"There is no secret, just do and be brave."
**William Orlowski, Tap Dancer and
Dance Choreographer**

~

The Feet of a Dancer

My daughter looked up at me at age two and uttered a single word. I no longer remember if it was "ballet" or "dance," but it set in motion years of taking her to dance classes of every genre, sewing costumes and watching performances. It didn't matter that she would grow to be six-feet tall, has little natural turnout and can't touch her toes. She has the soul of a dancer and loves being onstage. It's where she belongs.

Over the years she embraced almost every form of dance—tap, jazz, ballet, pointe, musical theater, modern and all forms of Polynesian dance. During her teenage years we found a studio that offered a flat monthly fee to take unlimited classes; she signed up for every one she could.

All her spare time for several years was spent in the studio training, and she performed in a whopping thirteen numbers in one season alone. Now an adult, she has answered that deep inner call by performing in a belly dance troupe.

All this, of course, cost money, and our budget was unbelievably tight. It wasn't just the studio fees—extra costs like costumes, competition fees and traveling expenses quickly added up. I needed to find a way to bring in extra dollars from home.

While I had only had a few sewing lessons in high school, I had sewn all my life. Offering to make dance costumes seemed to be the only door open. I could work from home and set my own hours.

Another costumer offered to help me get my foot in the door. I thought I would naturally start with beginner classes for children ages three to four. Instead, she talked one of the top dance schools into giving me a professional class, handed me a pattern she liked, patted me on the back and sent me out the door saying, "You can do it."

I was terrified as this wasn't what I bargained for. I thought I would start at the bottom and work my way up. Somehow I managed to deliver costumes that were well received. I was officially on the treadmill and I managed to hold on for five long years. Barely.

This was the most stressful job I had ever worked, and I wasn't well suited to the pressure. There were some great upsides, though, such as being at a dance competition with students from up to four schools performing in my creations. It was always a special moment when one of them would run up to me in a panic asking for help with their garment. I also proudly cheered them on as they performed from either the backstage or the audience.

Then there were the year-end shows where I sat in the audience glowing as I watched costume after costume I had personally sewn blend with the dancers' movements and the music to create something truly special.

Best of all, hands down, was getting to know all the students. I sewed for some of them for my entire five-year career. I watched them from their first class and followed them as they gained skill and confidence. They grew up as dancers, and as people, right in front of my eyes. I came to respect each and every one.

The closer we became and the more I sewed for them, the more in awe I was of these young, driven artists. The ones focused on a professional career in particular were so very strong. They gave up having a normal pre-teen and teen experience to focus fully on training. By high school many were only in academic schools for half days, spending from early afternoon until late in the evening training in the studio.

When I walked into the dressing room to do a fitting, it wasn't always filled with laughter. While it could be a noisy, fun space when recreational dancers were there, it could be pretty quiet when filled with serious semi-professionals. They would be spread around the limited space trying to get some studying done while doing their all-important stretching at the same time—school and dance prep walking hand in hand.

I still remember one young class that, because of their smaller stature, had to wait a little longer than usual to be introduced to those coveted pointe shoes.

Dancing *en pointe* is the holy grail for all serious ballet students, and tying on pointe shoes for the first time is their initiation to high level training. Could they be a professional one day? Starting *en pointe* was where the answer to that question would begin to be explored.

I had sewn for this particular group of talented students for several years. As they grew, I listened to them quietly express their hopes to start *en pointe* soon. I overhead their parents quietly reach out to teachers on the subject. When would their time come?

One day the news they had been waiting for so long magically arrived. They would begin to train *en pointe* in a few short weeks when the new dance semester began.

Elation radiated from every bone in their bodies. Their parents' faces glowed with pride. I happened to pop into the changing room the first week of their new pointe class and had to pause for a moment to soak in the joy around me.

A week or two later I was back in the studio to deal with a new costume order and again walked into the changing room. This time there was only silence. The dancers' somber expressions made it obvious that the reality, the physical cost, of dancing in pointe shoes had hit home.

For those who do not know—when en pointe, dancers are putting their full body weight on toes perched upon blocks of wood. Every movement takes its toll.

They were nursing extremely sore feet with several painful blisters—some broken and bleeding. Quietly they worked to get ready for their upcoming class—bandaging and massaging their poor battered feet, stretching sore muscles, tying on their beloved pointe shoes and trying to prepare themselves mentally for the coming physical challenges.

While it broke my heart as I wanted dance to be

something that always made their hearts sing, in looking from face to face I realized they were doing okay. They were strong.

I could clearly see sheer determination shining in each and every one of them. They would pay the price no matter what the physical cost as their dream was worth the sacrifice. Even the knowledge that only one or two at best would be good enough to join a company didn't discourage them. Simply having the chance to achieve their dream made it all worthwhile.

How could they have found that inner strength and driving passion at such a young age? It was beyond my comprehension.

From that moment until the day I walked away from sewing dance costumes, I inspected dancers' feet at every opportunity. It didn't matter what form of dance they were focused on. Blisters, bunions, corns, stress fractures, toes warped by being compressed in small shoes, bruises, numbness—a dancer's feet are never pretty. But let them step onto the stage and it all disappears. Magic happens.

The message I hope that comes through in this chapter is that embracing your passion doesn't always mean a joyful, carefree journey. There will be incredible highs, but there will also be devastating lows paired with unexpected and difficult challenges.

If what you do makes your heart sing, embrace it fully. Use that joy to carry you through. Know that the struggle to embrace your dreams is worth it, and that when you step onto life's stage you will forget all the negatives.

Magic will happen.

"Everyone wants to be successful until they see what it actually takes."
Unknown

"In life as in dance: Grace glides on blistered feet."
Alice Abrams, Ceramic Artist

~

Never Settle for Good Enough

One of the joys of becoming co-owner of a local fashion magazine early in my career was I had no expectations. I had no idea if there was a right or wrong approach to creating a publication. When I scheduled an interview so I could create content, I did so with a blank slate in front of me. I knew few details in advance about who the professional was or what their brand was about. Interviewing was simply a grand adventure—a leap into the unknown.

Every day I combed local newspapers, online media outlets and social media sites looking for fashion artists to add to my list of leads. Once a date and time were set, I made a point of doing little research ahead of time. Instead, I purposefully chose to arrive open and willing to hear whatever they chose to share.

Such was the case when I interviewed Patricia Fieldwalker. I had no idea she was an internationally recognized lingerie designer—already one of the top in the world for over three decades. I did not know celebrities such as Rihanna had been seen walking the streets wearing her beautiful designs or that they had been featured in movies.

I simply walked into her studio, totally oblivious and ready to hear her story.

My first reaction was to think how lovely it was to get to interview someone closer to my age. There is a mellowing and a focus that comes as the years pass that I am drawn to. Next was the powerful visual impact the beautiful garments hanging all around her studio had on me. I have sewn all my life and instantly recognized the quality of the luxurious silk and how perfect the shades in her chosen palette were.

Not once did I find myself thinking, "That's a little too…" or "If only she had…" Each garment was exactly the way it was meant to be and sewn impeccably to the highest tailoring standards. I could have sat there all day just soaking in the atmosphere.

As always, I started my interview with, "Where you born? Where did you grow up? What were you like as a child, as a teen? Looking back, can you remember anything, any moments that hinted you would embrace this career?" My goal is to draw out the story of their journey from the beginning to this moment in time with the interviewee in control, choosing what they personally feel is important to offer.

Patricia shared her story with an excited energy that let me know she was as passionate today as when she had first begun three decades earlier. I also quickly came to realize I was in the presence of a very successful artist.

She shared the amazing high of showing on the runway in Paris and the terrible low of having her business taken away, losing even the right to control her brand name. Lastly she talked about her journey to start all over again on a few old machines in an empty warehouse, building a new company from the ashes.

Among the many incredible moments throughout our interview, what I appreciated the most from this artist was the pride she took in her work. Every single detail of every single garment had to be perfect—the best silk, the best lace, difficult bias cuts so the garment would drape beautifully, the perfect silhouette, just the right hue and several truly talented seamstresses whose work was of the highest standard.

No shortcuts were allowed. If the garment needed ten tuck pleats to get the most beautiful fit, three wouldn't do. Mass production wouldn't do. Everything was made in-house in Patricia's small Vancouver atelier one at a time. Every single garment passed through her hands for approval and nothing was shipped unless it was absolutely the best it could be.

Each finished piece was also steamed until there wasn't a single wrinkle and hung on just the right hanger. Then it was carefully packaged for shipping in a way that meant it would arrive in exactly the same condition. Stockists could hang them right from the box.

At the time of this interview, the fashion industry was already heavily invested in mass production using cheap labor in poor countries. Even high-end stores like Saks were accepting garments constructed using lower standards out of fabrics that were not top quality.

Patricia was being pressured to do the same. Her answer was a resounding and unshakable "NO!" The lingerie she produced was a reflection of her values and would always be the best she could possibly create. Period.

That commitment to hold true to one's vision without letting it be undermined by outside forces really affected me. People were often telling me how to make money at writing by looking for popular topics and creating short articles based on them. I could choose to go that direction if it called me. But I also had the power to follow my instincts on what I wanted to offer. The choice was mine alone.

Patricia's story helped me realize that, like her, I honestly have no interest in creating work that is "popular" or "lucrative." I want to create the best work I can, writing created from my heart's passion. I want to offer others a glimpse into how truly wonderful and unique each of our lives is meant to be by sharing the journeys of others. I want to offer hope to anyone who is struggling.

Like Patricia, I choose not to let my work be compromised because of outside pressure. Instead I create work that makes my heart sing and I do it to the best of my ability. I have heard this wisdom echoed in many interviews since and it rings as true today as in that moment long ago.

"Do a good job. You don't have to worry about the money; it will take care of itself. Just do your best work and then try to trump it."
Walt Disney, Animator, Film Producer and Creator of The Walt Disney Company

One Step, One Moment, One Breath

I have shared previously that when I hear Sue Dumais of Heart Led Living speak, I always walk away with something new to consider. This was especially true during her appearance at Dream Talks 2016 in Vancouver.

Speaker after speaker took the stage to share their expertise with the audience. As always, I sat waiting for that telltale physical response that signals I need to listen carefully.

I truly believe that at every speaker series, there is one specific person I am there to hear. I also believe the reverse is true. For each speaker, there is at least one person in the audience who absolutely needs to receive what they have to offer.

My moment came when Sue took the stage.

She had recently returned from a trip to Africa where she had been connecting with women living in the Kibera Slum in Nairobi, Kenya. This was a fact-finding trip to try and figure out what was needed to help lift these women from their lives of poverty. Her local connection led her into the slums to meet several of these women and to hear in their own words about the future they desired and what they personally felt they needed to realize their dreams.

Walking through this squalid neighborhood was unpleasant. The homes were simple shacks thrown together with whatever materials were at hand. There was no power, no running water and no sewage system.

As Sue followed her local guide, she suddenly looked down and paused mid-step. Where should she put her foot down? The ground was a mix of water, mud and human waste. In that moment of indecision she heard the reassuring words of her guide telling her not to worry. Just take one step at a time.

Sharing this story again I still find myself affected. I also remember the first time I made a concentrated effort to embrace this wisdom.

My entry into the world of writing began in fashion, an industry I knew absolutely nothing about. Over time, others in the industry became close friends and I received tremendous support from them. I worked hard to return that support by offering media coverage.

I began attending Vancouver Fashion Week (VFW) in September 2007. Fashion weeks run twice a year—a Fall-Winter show and a Spring-Summer show. Each season, without fail, I attended this event to support the organizers and the designers showing their new collections.

From 4 p.m. onward I would be in my front-row seat watching every show. Then I would be up early the next morning to write up the shows from the day before, post by noon, share the link on social media, get ready and then head back downtown to do it all over again.

Over the next eight years VFW experienced tremendous

growth. Suddenly the coverage I offered which had been manageable in the past, became very large and overwhelming. To watch all of the shows I had to be in my seat for up to five hours a day over a six-day period with few breaks. Often I wouldn't arrive home until late in the evening—tired, hungry and wound up from all the excitement. Relaxing enough to fall asleep took time.

Each morning I was at the computer from 7 a.m. until noon writing my recaps. Then I had to get my articles posted, shared on social media, have lunch, dress, style my hair, apply makeup and head back downtown. By the end of each fashion week I would be exhausted and worn to a frazzle.

I loved being at the shows, immersed in a world of fashion artists showcasing their latest work. The energy is high and the excitement is palpable. The event also opened the door to building friendships with amazing designers from around the world. But the burden of offering the level of coverage I did, at a quality I could be proud of, was making it harder and harder for me to find the joy in being a part of this event.

The next VFW season was looming when I heard Sue's words that day—"one step at a time." They gave me hope that I could move through the demands I would soon be facing in a different way.

At a meeting of her Heart Led Living group not long after, she expanded on this topic. Sue began that day with the statement, "I don't do 'busy.'" Then she went on to explain no matter how full your schedule is on any given day, you don't need to stress. All you need to do to move through it peacefully and calmly is just be fully present in each moment, taking each step one at a time. No looking ahead or worrying about what is to come.

As I explored this idea and whether it had relevance in my life, my heart answered with a resounding "Yes."

Every aspect of what I wanted to accomplish during VFW could be broken down into single moments to move through. Choosing what to wear, getting ready, driving to the event, writing up the shows the next morning and posting on social media were each relegated to their own moment, with no thought of what I had done before or what I had to do next.

While driving to the venue, I no longer worried about whether I would arrive in time. I embraced the drive just as it was—enjoying the scenery, listening to music and allowing myself to be patient with any delays.

Over the next few days I began to notice a lack of stress. I arrived at the venue relaxed and looking forward to any inspiration I might receive from the day's shows, my heart wide open to any new people I might have the privilege to meet that day.

As I turned my focus away from my deadlines and instead made an effort to simply be fully present in each moment, my anxiety began to fade away. I found that by allowing a single thought to be developed instead of juggling twenty at once, completing each day's write-up took far less time. Instead of barely finishing by noon, I was done by 10 a.m.

Thinking about what was ahead and how much I needed

to get done had always caused me a lot of worry. What I learned that week was that we can get so much more done without working any harder by giving all our attention to what we are doing in that moment. Looking ahead or behind simply slows us down.

I would love to say I have fully integrated this wisdom and that it's now second nature, but the fact is this simple truth will most likely be a lifelong journey of rediscovery for me. Every time I find myself getting anxious, I have to take a moment to slow down, breathe and remind myself I only need to take whatever is on my plate that day one step, one moment, one breath at a time.

We are each unique. Perhaps you are someone who thrives surrounded by chaos. Or perhaps you are someone who is always worried you won't finish in time. Maybe you yo-yo between the two.

Wherever you are on the spectrum, I suggest you try setting aside a single hour one day. Pick just one thing you would like to spend your time on and let go of what lies ahead. Embrace being fully present in that moment doing this one single thing.

I promise it will be an eye opener.

> *"You can't get it right. You can't get it wrong. [Life] just is. You only need to be present."*
> **Sue Dumais, Founder of Heart Led Living**

Permission to Do Nothing

This chapter is very connected to the last. While the two could have been combined, I felt each deserved to stand on its own as the concepts are complimentary but unique.

The previous one focuses on dealing with a full schedule. This chapter explores allowing empty moments regardless of your schedule, something we all need.

Look around you. We live in a crazy world running at top speed. Cell phones are now attached to our bodies like unwelcome growths. They sit on the table between us as we try to connect over coffee or lunch, interrupting our attempts to have a conversation. Book after book and speaker after speaker offer advice on the subject of how to get more done in a day. It is the rare voice that says, "Do nothing."

Life used to be much harder in previous centuries. People had to grow their own food, make their own clothes and work morning to night just to survive. We are blessed today to have free time to use simply for our enjoyment.

Whether you participate in a sport, try yoga, learn to paint, take up an instrument or travel, these are joys that many who came before us didn't have the opportunity to embrace. So why do so many of us feel stretched to the limit?

Society today rarely encourages downtime and the word "should" creeps in far too often. If you read a book, it *should* be motivational, offer wisdom on how to move your business forward or be one you can review on your blog. Free time *should* be spent getting in shape at the gym, attending an event to network with others or participating in an activity.

Restaurants where I live now set the volume high on background music, making it hard to hear even the person next to you. It's almost as though they're afraid to let us relax. We need to be pumped up to enjoy ourselves.

With the help of my mentor Sue, I began to consider allowing myself at times to choose to do nothing. Though it shouldn't have come as such a surprise, it proved to be another truth that hit me profoundly. This was a revolutionary concept in my world; it flew in the face of what society was telling me.

I think the first time I heard Sue talk on the subject of doing nothing, the story went something like this. She was working on her business at the computer and suddenly felt guided to stretch out on the couch and rest. Two hours later she arose, sat back down at the same computer and completed a sale.

What? Many of us would have pounded away at making that sale and maybe, just maybe, allowed ourselves the luxury of some downtime after this achievement as a reward for being such a great worker and sticking with it. Letting go of the idea of rest and relaxation only as a reward for working hard seemed extraordinary.

As I explored the concept more, I began to notice a pattern in the world around me.

When we push ourselves too hard or stretch ourselves too thin without allowing enough time to relax, our bodies respond in a way that can't be ignored. We get sick or hurt. That simple physical revolt forces us to pull back for a bit of time at least and take care of ourselves. It gives us permission to ignore the societal pressure to always be achieving.

Once you notice a truth, you start to see it popping up all around you. It's like a pebble dropped in a pond creating a series of ripples.

Suddenly I was drawn to more sources of information on self-care and constantly being reminded how important it is to create health in my own life before I move out into the world. The idea that the best way to create success is from a place of peace and health arose over and over again. It was also becoming clear to me that downtime was an important part of the equation.

As I embraced this idea, my personal stress began to lessen. I quit brow-beating myself if I didn't cross everything off my to-do list each day. In fact, I eventually quit writing a to-do list.

There were times I chose, without apology, to curl up with a great fiction book and enjoy reading. Other wonderful, rejuvenating moments arose when I felt led to reach out to friends and have coffee or chose to spend time with my husband.

There are still many days I work hard for hours on end,

but my heart now clearly leads me to see when this is the right choice and when it is time to walk away. Finding balance has become a priority, and at times that means simply doing nothing. I don't need permission or have to have completed a certain amount of work to justify taking some time to myself.

Take time this week to think about your schedule and how you move through each day. Do you allow yourself quiet moments to hear your inner voice? Are you open to hearing any truth that might be offered, even if it says it's time for self-care? Can you be brave enough to give yourself permission to have a few hours, or even a few days, when you do nothing but rest?

If allowing yourself time to do nothing is a struggle for you, then release the word "nothing." Nothing is a poor description anyway. Call it time off or a "daycation." Your body needs regular breaks so it can regenerate, and your mind needs time off to refresh. It's an important part of building health mentally, spiritually and physically.

If someone asks you what you did one day when it was one filled with much-needed downtime, simply answer with truth, "I took some time for myself." Embrace it. Say it without guilt. You deserve it.

"Taking time to do nothing often brings everything into perspective."
Doe Zantamata, Author, Artist and Photographer

The Bicycle Story

Sometimes wisdom is handed to me while listening to a new interview, to a speaker or when reading a great book. Other times it comes in small bites—a little one here, a little one there. Slowly the individual bites accumulate in my subconscious until occasionally a brand new idea bursts into my awareness. The bicycle story came about just this way.

There seem to be two conflicting schools of thought on how to approach goals, whether business or personal. Is it best to embrace the long or the short view when deciding on a new direction?

Those who embrace the long view encourage us to make vision boards, create to-do lists, set long-term goals and write everything, including individual deadlines, on a calendar. Each day we need to keep our eyes on the future so we can stay on the right path.

Those who embrace the contrasting approach, the short view, encourage us to let our intuition guide us, to live fully in each moment. As long as we're putting one foot in front of the other, our inner voice will lead us to walk the path we are meant to be on.

I struggled with these conflicting ideas for a very long

time. If I focused on the future, I often found myself caught up in worrying about deadlines and whether I was getting enough done. The schedules I set were often unrealistic. This caused a lot of guilt and stress and often resulted in me berating myself for not achieving what I set out to do.

If I turned my focus to just being fully present in each moment, the stress and guilt disappeared but it felt like an element was missing. Without at least some idea of my long-term goals, it was too easy to get sidetracked and accomplish nothing. Without looking at my calendar at least occasionally, I sometimes forgot appointments.

There had to be a way to unite the two.

In 2014, I pulled out my bicycle and started riding for the first time in twenty years. Why? My husband is an avid cyclist, and we decided to book two bike excursions as part of our upcoming trip to Prague, Vienna and Budapest. This would be a challenge for me, but I was ready and willing to put in some time training.

The first few weeks were really tough. I couldn't cycle very far and my backside didn't take kindly to sitting on that torturous seat. Day by day my endurance improved until I was riding a full 12.5 miles each time out.

The summer was beautiful that year and over the next four months of preparation, I began to look forward to the feeling of flying down the road with the sun on my face and the wind in my hair. There were also unexpected benefits.

I was writing my first book at the time and struggling with debilitating self-doubt. I learned in tough moments to jump up, grab my bike and head off for an hour of hard exercise. By the time I arrived back at the computer my mind would be clear, the stress washed out of my system and the words I had been seeking seemed to sort themselves out. All I had to do was sit down and capture them on the computer.

There was one more benefit to my newfound hobby: a profound life lesson that caught me off guard.

One struggle I had while riding was when I had to go between the barrier posts that are common at the entrance of combined walking/cycling paths. Every time I approached a set of those dreaded posts, panic would set in. The closer I came, the more I slowed down. I couldn't take my eyes off them. This, of course, drew me toward them like a magnet. I would swerve crazily and nearly crash every single time.

When I mentioned this problem to my husband he offered the perfect solution. "Don't focus on the posts. Focus on something ahead." It sounded way too simple, but I was game to give it a try.

I still vividly remember the next time I was out riding. There was a tree standing a few hundred feet past my nemesis, so I chose to focus one hundred percent on the tree instead of what was in front of my wheels. Miraculously I sailed right between those previously scary barriers at full speed without a care in the world.

After a few months of embracing this new and freeing focus, I began to realize it had something to teach me in terms of my personal journey. We often get so distracted by what we perceive as barriers to our goals that we spend all our energy worrying about how they could stop us from succeeding.

Unfortunately, what we focus on is usually what we manifest in our life.

If this is where you are, just for one day give yourself permission to let go of all the doubts and negativity around you. Look ahead without distraction at the wide-open door of possibilities just waiting for you to walk through. Picture a bright future filled with images of you doing the things you love.

For the most part I choose to live one day at a time, one step at a time, one moment at a time, one breath at a time—being fully present and focused. It allows me to work faster as I only have my mind on a single task instead of thinking about everything I need to accomplish. This keeps my soul in a peaceful place.

However, I've learned when it comes to my dreams for the future, I take the long view and don't worry about what comes between this moment and reaching them. I ride toward them full speed without a care, embracing any detours or changes in direction that come along the way with ease.

"Life is like riding a bicycle. To keep your balance, you must keep moving."
Albert Einstein, Scientist

~

What Relationship Do You Want with Your Clothing?

When I first stepped into the role of media covering local fashion I was pretty far outside my comfort zone. Fashion was something I'd never had a lot of time or money to explore.

At that point in my life my clothing came from discount department stores, Costco and thrift shops. Shoes were usually bought at inexpensive shoe rack outlets or purchased through eBay and Amazon. My husband cut my hair.

Money was tight. The cost of a garment drove my purchases rather than whether it was a quality purchase that would last.

I lucked into working with Shannon, a wonderful stylist who over time helped me build my wardrobe from the ground up. The goal was to add a few quality garments each season that would last a long time and complement previous purchases. Slowly my wardrobe started to come together and people noticed the change. My confidence grew.

During the time I began to work on my first book, I reached out to Katherine Soucie of Sans Soucie Textile and Design. She was one of my initial interviews back when I first began this writing career. Our personal and professional relationship had grown in wonderful ways over the years and it was always exciting when a new opportunity arose for me to write about her work

Even though I had multiple recordings on file, I never could resist the chance to sit with her again one-on-one. This would be our fourth interview. But no matter how many times she shared her journey, I was always ready to explore uncharted territory and perhaps learn something new.

This time around I had the chance to ask more about her young years and to take a more personal look into her journey building a brand that stands out as unique on the Eco fashion stage—not an easy feat to achieve. The fashion industry is filled with designers, each trying to become household names. Students graduating from fashion design programs each year are added to the already large numbers of artists working in the industry.

For the first time, I discovered how deep her connection to her production machines went. Most had been discarded because they were out of date. She embraced them, repurposed them and gave them dinosaur names in tribute—extinct creatures given a new life.

Katherine also shared in greater depth about how the fashion industry as it now stands is not sustainable. The throw-away mentality encouraged by the industry squanders both money and resources, and it creates large amounts of waste that contribute to pollution. There needs to be a shift in focus to buying fewer, higher quality garments that will last.

Then came the statement that would occupy my thoughts for the next six months, "We as consumers need to decide what relationship we want with our clothing."

If the fashion industry is a foreign beast to you, these words might not have the same impact. I had been immersed in it for a good eight years at this point, but I was still a bit of an outsider. I really didn't care about seasons or trends; for me, it was all about the artist's journey to this moment and how they expressed themselves through their brand.

However, being immersed in the fashion world meant I was painfully aware of the terrible cost of current industry practices and the sheer amount of discards that hit landfills each year.

Over the next six months I found myself at random times walking into my closet and looking at the garments hanging there. Which drew my eyes? Which brought a smile to my face? Why? What would I change? In the end I came to realize what I wanted to have in my closet was clothing that had meaning for me—a story I could share about why I cherished each garment.

Perhaps the story might be that I had interviewed the designer or heard about them in the media and supported what they were doing. Maybe their journey or the story behind their collection was intriguing. The story could also be something unique about the design, the fabric or how I came to purchase it.

My heart sings when someone notices a treasured garment I am wearing. As an added bonus, their remark usually opens the door to a lively conversation and sometimes, a fabulous new connection.

In talking with designer and producer Denise Brillon of Artifaax on this topic, I came to realize these items with stories were my regalia—cherished garments that hold a personal significance to me as a fashion writer. I only wear them at special times and I feel a sense of pride and a connection with the designer when I wear them.

Because I cherish them, I treat them with great care and I enthusiastically share their story every chance I get. They are not seasonal fad purchases, discarded when styles change. They are treasures that will stay in my wardrobe for a very long time.

Over the next few months, spend a few moments here and there to think about what relationship you want with your clothing. Take your time, there is no rush. There is no one right response. You are unique and that will be reflected in your personal answer.

There are items in my closet that aren't regalia—my pajamas, my exercise clothes, the ones I cook in and the ones I clean house in. That's okay. Don't worry about being overly strict or rigid. Not every piece of clothing needs to be meaningful or purposeful.

If your relationship is just about wearing the latest look, give yourself permission. If it's a certain color palette, that's fine too. Whatever you discover will be meaningful to you alone.

Once you understand the relationship you want, what and how you add to your closet will change. Decisions will no longer be made impulsively by what the media tells you is in style this season. You'll also likely find yourself buying less. Purchases will come to be made by what you are drawn to, and you'll end up with a wardrobe full of treasured possessions.

> *"When you don't dress like everybody else, you don't have to think like everybody else .... You have to look in the mirror and see yourself.*
> **Iris Apfel, Businesswoman, Interior Designer and Fashion Icon**

~

Hold Open the Door of Possibility

I can't even read the title of this chapter without getting a physical reaction; it's that powerful for me.

Every time I attend a daylong series of speakers, I find myself wondering what I am there to learn. Who will take the stage and offer me something new I can go on to share with others?

In January 2016, I had the privilege of attending the first-ever PowHERtalks Vancouver. Eighteen women took the stage, each speaking for eight minutes on a subject dear to their heart. Every single one offered welcome wisdom and insight, but that day my moment came during a talk called "The Crazy Naked Truth," given by Mental Health Speaker, Bi-Polar Princess and CEO of Crazy for Life Co., Victoria Maxwell.

Victoria opened by sharing what the audience at first thought was just a humorous story. We all sat up just a bit taller when this story ended with her being taken by the police to the psych ward. It turned out she was in the middle of a manic episode searching for God.

What followed was a heartfelt sharing covering her journey with bipolar disorder—from diagnosis to acceptance to health. Despite the heavy subject, most of the time she managed to tell her story in a way that brought a smile to our faces. However, it was very difficult to hear about the negativity, judgment and dismissive attitude that came from others.

Those who did not understand her condition sometimes reacted with embarrassment or scorn. Even in the hospital, professionals would talk about her like a problem to be dealt with instead of a human being. She overheard staff referring to her using adjectives like "crazy." On the other side of the equation were many people who cared and made the road she traveled easier.

It took Victoria several years to accept that she had a problem and to embrace the better future offered. What made the most difference in her journey were the people who understood what was needed and accepted the challenge.

Victoria had a supportive family that stood by her side. She also had a wonderful counselor who didn't deny her reality. He chose to step into her world and accept the way she experienced each day. Over time he helped open her eyes to what her future could hold.

At this point she shared a key and a very powerful message. The people who made the most difference in her life were the ones who held open the door of possibility for her until she was strong enough to hold it open herself, until she was ready to walk through the door and embrace those opportunities.

Stop for a moment and read that sentence again because it's very important.

The people who made the most difference in her life were the ones who held open the door of possibility for her until she was strong enough to hold it open herself, until she was ready to walk through the door and embrace those opportunities.

For me, it was an eye opener. Victoria helped me realize it wasn't up to me to convince someone there was a better way of doing things. I didn't have to find a way to fix everyone's problems, to get them to see things in the "right" way or to make them embrace a life I felt was better for them.

All that was needed of me was to simply step into their world without judgment, to fully embrace them just as they are in that moment of time, to offer them love and support, to cherish them without expectations and hold open the door of possibility so they can see what their future could be.

Next came a truth that was hard to hear.

We all want to think if we love, cherish, step into their world without judgment and hold open the door of possibility, those we love will always choose to walk through it. Unfortunately, this isn't always the case.

We can't force someone to take that step. All we can do is hold a safe and supportive space for them. The decision is theirs, and we need to respect whatever choice they make.

In reflecting on my journey to become a published author, I see this same trend. Long before I could begin to accept that I was good enough to actually finish the rough draft of my first book, there were people around me who held open that door of possibility for me.

They believed in my ability and that I could embrace this

future. They held that vision for me in low times; in high times, they celebrated with me when I finally chose to walk through the door and embrace my dream. I have serious doubts I would have been able to accomplish finishing my first book without their unwavering support.

Intrigued? A video of this wonderful talk is available on PowHER TV Media's YouTube station under the title PowHERtalks | Victoria Maxwell. I highly recommend setting a few moments aside to watch it.

> *"It's amazing what people will do when you see the best in them, when you honor them, when you respect them. It not only strengthens the relationship, but it will help that other person rise higher."*
> **Joel Osteen, Author**

~

Money Is Not My Motivation

In recent years I've seen a rising push toward entrepreneurship. There are many reasons for this trend including the climate created by an increasingly difficult job market, the draw of wider career choices, greater personal control and more financial opportunity. Women in particular can struggle to reach the upper levels of management in some companies or find their options—and wages—limited after taking time off to focus on family.

While I understand and support the desire to be an entrepreneur for all who love running their own business, I am concerned with what seems to be an unwavering focus on money as the end goal. We are encouraged to monetize every single thing we do, and those who don't follow through on this are greeted with a raised eyebrow (or two).

Every women's group and speaker series I've attended in the last year has emphasized the success side of business heavily. I have struggled to find very many in support of those of us who look at what we do from the perspective of artistic expression and passion. This is especially true for authors.

Publishing a book has become one of the most highly

recommended marketing tools for entrepreneurs. Being an author labels you as an expert in your field and can open many doors. For these authors, the focus is on the exposure a book can get you. Advice is given on how to publish profitably and when it makes sense to give the books away for free to prospects as a marketing tool. The support these authors need is quite different and very specific.

Those of us who write from passion can feel isolated. There are support groups that help with daily accountability, but most author workshops focus on economics. All writers would like to make money or at least break even, but the market has become extremely competitive. Self-publishing and hybrid-publishing have made it harder than ever for an author to get noticed, especially with his or her first book.

As of May 20, 2016, Amazon was offering 33,969,607 paperbacks on their site. Add in ebooks and that number rises even higher. The difficulties of navigating this new reality is distracting to say the least. I often find myself overwhelmed with the need to focus on marketing. Somehow the joy of creating new work gets lost in the process.

Everyone working in the arts is drawn here by our desire to create. We choose to walk this path because we have something bubbling from deep within that needs expression. When it's also our paycheck, the shift can quickly become far more on business than on creativity. We have to be both an entrepreneur and an artist.

Not everyone can switch between these two opposing

roles easily. With little time spent oiling our creative gears, the whole process can become stifled. Balancing these two roles is definitely a huge challenge for me personally.

The journey to embracing my career as an author began with my deep desire to hear others share about their lives. To book any interview, I had to assure my prospect I would publish a written article. At first it was sheer hard work to take their words and create a finished piece that would be acceptable for publication, but over time I came to love the process of writing as well.

Next came the realization of my purpose—giving wings to the stories of others.

I came to feel strongly that in this day and age, when many are heavily influenced by reality television, the world needs to be offered better role models to guide us. I wanted to create a platform for people to share their life's journey— the highs and the lows—and to pass on the lessons they have learned.

My hope when sharing these stories is that they will inspire people to embrace their passion, to understand that their quirks are their talents, to give them permission to walk their own unique path and to help promote diversity as a strength and as something to be celebrated.

This is my passion and the reason I continue to embrace writing as a career.

After releasing my first book, I breathed a huge sigh of relief. I thought I was done. Writing that book had also inspired me to write down five new title ideas that I dreamed would also become published books. A few weeks off and I figured I'd be ready to start in on book two.

After a few days though, I realized that the hard work had only just begun. I needed to market my first book, a journey that consumed my time for the next year and a half.

I continued to write articles and do blogs posts, but there just didn't seem to be enough time or energy left over to write the new books that were calling to me. Most groups I explored only reinforced that I needed to figure out how to promote my work, monetize my blog and manage my time better, as well as emphasizing the importance of marketing myself better by becoming a speaker.

While I don't object to any of those goals, what was missing was an understanding of what I was ultimately trying to achieve. Where could I find support simply for my journey as an artist?

Writing is not about money for me. Even if I never make a dime, I will always be glad I chose to walk this path and be extremely proud of the work I have produced. What I write comes from my heart. It is my passion.

I have struggled through debilitating self-doubt and sleepless nights to get to this point, each step along the way supported by amazing friends and a loving family. I laughed, I cried and I almost gave it all up on one dark night.

Would I like to be financially successful? Yes. That would mean I could continue to publish new titles and perhaps enjoy a nice holiday here and there. However, money has never been my motivation. I am simply driven to write.

My hope is that the words I share will make a difference in someone else's life.

I stand fully ready to embrace success, but determined to not lose myself in the process. First and foremost, my writing is my purpose and my passion. It is my artistic expression and I intend to keep it that way.

Just as I was getting ready to finish this chapter, I saw a poster that resonated on this subject called "Ten Signs You're Doing Well in Life." I decided to use it as a basis for a list of my own.

- I wake up each morning to a new day.
- I have a roof over my head.
- I'm double blessed—this roof is on a home I love.
- I live in a country that offers me freedom and protections others do not have.
- I have food to eat each and every day.
- I have clothes to wear that fulfill all my needs.
- I have the love of my husband and family, and my children are all doing well.
- I am a good friend and mentor to those in my circle.
- I have the support of many wonderful friends and business associates.
- I have many dreams to pursue and countless opportunities to explore.
- I have the ability to embrace my passion —interviewing.

As you walk your own unique journey, always remember to notice and be thankful for the little things. In the end they are often the most important.

There will be times to consider the finances and times to consider your purpose and passion. It's okay to embrace financial success; just make sure your decisions aren't driven by the money side of the equation alone.

There is so much more to your success than just a dollar sign.

"Be fearless in the pursuit of what sets your soul on fire."
Jennifer Lee, Screenwriter and Director

~

Do You Love It Enough to Make It Your Job?

Are you thinking of turning your passion or your hobby into a business? If so, this question is one you should take a moment to consider before taking that leap. Do you love it enough to make it your job?

With over a hundred and fifty full-life interviews behind me, the one thing each person interviewed has made clear is that when anything becomes your business, it can quickly become ninety percent hard work and ten percent what you love to do. This certainly rang true for me.

When I began writing, all I had to do was book an interview, transcribe the recording, write the article and submit it for publication. I loved interviewing, but was annoyed by the rest. Transcribing the recording was a very valuable experience as I was still learning how to focus and listen without making assumptions, but I found it truly boring. Writing became easier over time, but in the beginning the process of learning how to write an article was hard work.

From day one I chose to send my finished piece to the interviewee to get their comments before publishing. Why? Because time after time I heard during interviews about how other writers had made mistakes in their articles and how upsetting that was for my subjects.

My interviewees' feedback was sometimes hard to receive, but became an important part of building my reputation. I wanted them to know I cared about getting the story right. I took to heart every suggestion and criticism, but I would not write anything that was in any way inaccurate. It was a time-consuming process.

In the beginning, every time I had the privilege of sharing someone's journey with the world I worried when I sent them the draft to review. Did I get it right? Sometimes the answer was yes—other times it was a discouraging no. The process wasn't always easy, but after about a year I began to realize the blessing of receiving difficult feedback.

Although their criticism was hard to hear, each bit of negative feedback offered me an opportunity to improve my listening skills, to understand where I missed the mark, to recognize the important truth behind what they shared and to become better at writing a story that rings true.

This is a process I still go through today, and the feedback I receive continues to help me improve as a writer.

When I began co-running a local magazine and working for another a year later, my focus shifted from writing to fulfilling my responsibilities. For the local magazine in particular, I had to find time to hire, train and manage new writers; acquire leads; set up schedules; sell ads to finance an annual print edition; and circulate the hard copies once they arrived.

My personal interviewing and writing began to take a

back seat to all the other responsibilities that landed on my desk. Creativity was left in the past. Putting words to paper simply became work that needed to get done. Fortunately by then I had the skill set in place to make it happen.

Days sometimes stretched late into the evening and the pressure felt heavy on my shoulders. I began to wonder if things would ever quiet down to the point I could again enjoy the process of interviewing and writing.

One of my lovely fashion friends, Pam, reached out to schedule a coffee date at the perfect moment. She planted a seed that day that would grow over the next year to have a huge impact on my journey as a writer, taking me in a whole new direction.

I shared with her my frustration with the lack of creativity in my work—how business had taken over and writing had become just a job. She suggested I start a personal blog. I'm still embarrassed to share that I instantly scoffed at her suggestion. Up to this point, all of the blogs I had seen featured a lot of pictures accompanied by just tiny bits of writing. What was she thinking?

Pam assured me my blog could be whatever I needed it to be. I didn't have to worry about how many followers I had or if anyone was reading my articles. I could just use it as a safe space to write personal thoughts and explore a wider variety of topics.

Over the next few days the idea continued to bubble up until I threw caution to the wind. I launched "Olio by Marilyn" in August 2010.

Why did I choose the word "olio" for my title? "Olio"

refers to a miscellaneous collection—like an assortment of oddities or a mish mash of unrelated things. I had no plans to build this site into a themed blog on a specific topic. All I wanted was a place to share whatever thoughts came to mind and to be able to change directions on a whim. "Olio" described that beautifully.

In the beginning my articles were all about writing for pleasure. No topic was off limits. Surprisingly it started to build a readership. I was so enamored of what it was becoming, I chose to spend some of my limited funds to have a logo created by Adrian, a local graphic artist I trusted. I had no ideas to offer; I just left the creative process fully in his capable hands. You'll find it proudly displayed at the end of most chapters.

The blog became very important on the very day my career took a sharp turn in an unexpected way. The magazine I had co-founded folded in 2012. I was devastated by the loss of something I had poured so much of myself into. I was left feeling adrift—like a boat on the open ocean with no sail, motor or anchor.

What followed was a dark time for me. After four and a half years spent putting everything I had into trying to build a magazine I was proud of and that stood out as unique in the industry, it was gone in an instant. To make things worse, I had allowed all of my personal branding as a writer to become tied to the magazines I worked for. Perhaps it was time to let go of my dream and move on.

Deep inside, though, I could still hear a small voice asking me to reconsider, so I made a decision. I would write a new article every day for six weeks and publish them on my blog. At the end of this time, I'd take another look at what my future might hold. This became a lifeline for the passion that continued to call me.

Each morning I'd grab a cup of coffee, write for from fifteen minutes to an hour, do a quick edit and then hit "publish" before I lost my courage. Subjects such as my relationship with my mother, driving in traffic, a story inspired by a word of the day, a personal experience, recipes I tried and even throwing up found their way onto my blog's digital pages. Every time I hit "publish" and shared my latest article on social media, I fanned the dying flames of my original passion a little higher.

At the end of six weeks I still had no idea where I would head next as a writer, but I was committed to finding out. It was then I heard Julie Salisbury speak on her publishing workshop. Immediately I knew this was the answer.

What I discovered shortly after I proudly launched my first book is that reaching publication is only the beginning. Marketing takes time and effort. There was so much to learn and the competition to break through and find a solid group of committed readers is fierce. You have to constantly discover new ways to keep yourself and your book in the public eye. The marketing work was, and still is, exhausting.

It has taken two years for me to finally move to a place where I am again spending the largest amount of my time on writing. However, that balance will probably tip heavily back in the other direction each time I release a new book.

Without marketing, I can't properly share these wonderful stories, and I am committed to helping my books fly high and go far.

Do I love it enough to make it my job? I still ask myself this question on a regular basis. So far the answer continues to be "Yes." Interviewing and writing are still my passion and purpose.

If I ever feel a hesitation or hear a no, then I know it will be time to consider what might be next on my journey and try to discover what new doors are standing open ready to welcome me.

"Working hard for something we don't care about is called stress. Working hard for something we love is called passion."
Simon Sinek, Author, Motivational Speaker and Marketing Consultant

~

Creating a Recipe for Success

One day I was approached to create a thirty-to forty-minute video course. The company offering me this new opportunity was also open to a wide range of topics. It was up to me what the subject and content would be. The company would film it and then I would profit share on the rental fees they collected when someone viewed my video.

While this opportunity fell through in the end, it was a great chance to think about what should be in such a course and to develop it as a possible speaking topic. I decided to include an overview of the outline I created for this course here, because it reinforces some of the ideas I've been sharing in previous chapters–an echo to bring the message home again.

Creating a recipe for success really begins with your passion and your why. It's the most important place to start. What is it you really want from life? On your death bed, what do you want to be able to say you've accomplished—personally and professionally? These are important questions to consider.

I think most of us, if we're being completely honest, would admit we would like to enjoy some measure of financial security. Food on the table and a roof over our heads are wonderful things as well. But when it comes to accomplishments, I'm not sure a dollar figure is the first thing that comes to mind.

Family, friends, love, travel—there is a lot more to our dreams than just money.

Take a moment right now and clear your mind. Try to calm the flood of thoughts. In that quiet and safe space, let your intuition consider what it is that matters most to you. There is no wrong answer. Just let the ideas bubbling up come into focus without judgment. You might be surprised.

The next step is to look at these ideas and see which draws you the most. Don't discard the others. Over your lifetime your passions may change. You could move in a new direction many times if you stay open to the possibilities. For now, though, just listen for where you feel led to start.

What quirks are stirring at the thought of this new direction? Could this be the garden they've been waiting to be planted in? Interviewing was my first step, but it was only one of many leading me to new experiences I could not have even conceived in the beginning.

Now is the time to ask yourself a couple of questions I heard TV personality, fashion editor and author Jeanne Beker once share. A young woman ran up to her in public one day and enthused, "I want your job." Her response, said with great humor was, "Get your own job."

What she meant is this young woman should have dreams bigger than just repeating what Jeanne had created over her twenty-year career. She needed to make her own individual mark.

Jeanne encouraged the young woman to ask herself, "What new idea can I bring to the table?" Doing what had been done before wouldn't allow her to showcase her own unique talents. She should direct her energy toward creating something original and exciting.

Every time I am asked to meet with young entrepreneurs who want to launch yet another digital fashion magazine, I try to steer the conversation to these questions. "Is what you want to create just a repetition of what's already out there? What new and interesting idea can you bring to a digital fashion magazine to set you apart from the crowd?"

Dare to be different and take a new direction.

Patricia Fieldwalker has a lot to say on this subject. She actually fell into becoming an international icon offering luxury lingerie the day she decided to create a quality camisole for herself. Back then everything in the stores was cheap and mass-produced. In comparison, what she created exhibited an utterly luxurious standard. People noticed and orders began to come in.

From day one she held firm to a brand offering only luxury garments made one at a time by highly skilled seamstresses in her small atelier. The pressure to accept the shift to a lower quality, mass-produced product increased each and every year; but unless she was proud of her work, she refused to put it out there. She would not be swayed.

Before you begin is also the perfect time to consider whether you truly want to take something that gives you pleasure and turn it into a serious business. Remember that ninety-ten split I mentioned in "Do You Love It

Enough to Make It Your Job?" In the beginning at least, you will spend only ten percent of your time doing what you love. The other ninety percent will be spent building your business. The journey ahead will involve lots of hard work and a roller coaster ride of incredible highs and dark lows.

If at this point you decide you'd rather keep this passion as something for your spare time, that's okay. Exploring all possibilities is a great way to slowly hone in on a new direction.

Take your time. Be willing to change course whenever you feel guided to do so.

As you move forward, there is a time for long-term planning and a time for being in the moment. Each has its place. Long-term planning might include acquiring the skills you'll need either through schooling, apprenticeship or hiring the right team. Luxury show designer Ruthie Davis worked for three other companies before launching her own brand.

Finding a mentor who is capable of giving strong but unbiased feedback is also a good idea. And as much as we'd all love a new business idea to quickly become a reality, giving your concept the time it needs to fully develop is extremely important.

Perfumer Geir Ness did both. He chose to work with a retired perfumer who had years of industry experience to create his beautiful scent. He took to heart this expert's advice on how to begin, spent the time needed to test market and adjust the scent and patiently listened to his mentor's feedback as his scent begin to take shape. The process was long, a full five years from start to finish. But when "Laila" was finalized, he launched it to great acclaim.

From the moment you say yes to this journey, you need to build your social media presence. And if you haven't begun building your ujamaa tribe yet, this is also a priority. Building a community around you isn't just about support—it's also about who needs what you are offering. It's about giving from your heart and sharing your passion to make their world better.

Every morning when you get up, embrace joy in the knowledge that you are able to do what you love. Allow yourself to ignore any negativity coming your way and keep your eyes open wide. New opportunities can arise at any moment.

Try not to be so focused on the future or your to-do list that you miss being in the moment. Being fully present in each moment during your day will actually allow you to see what the universe may be offering. Where you are headed could take an unexpected turn in a new direction—one you couldn't even have imagined. I love to call this "turning left" when it happens to me. Be ready to leap.

I want to wrap up this chapter with a few key points I've learned over my decade of interviewing

Key Points

- Never stop learning. Every day holds great adventures in wisdom.

- There will never be a moment you are finished. There will always be a new piece of gold ready to change your life.

- Persistence and patience do pay off, but they most likely will take time. Don't let yourself get discouraged when things don't come together right away.

- Do your research, study each issue from all angles and then quiet your mind. Clear it of all distraction and let your inner voice speak to you. It will process everything in a creative way, guiding your journey with ideas and solutions your more rigid intellect couldn't conceive.

- Look the part. You don't have to have a big expensive wardrobe assembled by a stylist, but it's important to live and breathe what you represent in all areas of your life. It not only helps others who meet you to understand where you are coming from, it helps you embrace the role. Dressing in a way that is in alignment with who you are puts you firmly into your role mentally before you step out the door. It's a real confidence booster.

- No one succeeds in a vacuum. No one succeeds alone. Surround yourself with a good team whether just one person or many.

"You have to really love what you do, because it's not a career, it's a love affair."
Patricia Fieldwalker, Luxury Lingerie Designer

"Never stop working on your skills and expertise. Never stop learning. Each day gives you new opportunities."
Geir Ness, Creator of "Laila," The Essence of Norway

"Even in the face of challenge, it's important to find the courage to live a life of purpose. When you live a life of purpose and share it with the world, it awakens and inspires others to do the same."
Pamela Masik, Artist

"I've been doing this for forty years and still haven't mastered my trade. But if I did master it, what would I do then?"
Martin Jackson, Master Calligrapher

"By choosing to embrace your mission and let it lead you where it may, life becomes a daring and, dare I say, an exciting adventure!"
Caroline MacGillivray, Beauty Night Society Founder

"There are moments in your life where, if that moment didn't happen, the rest of your life would have taken a totally different direction."
Lisa Marie Mazzucco, Photographer

~

Giving Birth to a Book

The idea to write an article titled "The Paperback Pregnancy" came to me one day while behind the wheel driving to who knows where. I no longer remember how my train of thought led me randomly from book writing back to pregnancy, but the similarities made me smile.

As soon as I arrived home, I sat down and penned a rough draft in less than an hour. The words just flowed and I found myself laughing as I wrote. It's still one of my favorite blog posts.

Then last night as I was dozing off, the idea arose to include the article in this book. At first I discarded the notion. Does this really fit in with the rest of the content? Maybe not, but my heart continued to speak and would not be denied.

Knowing how my mind works, I knew sleep would be elusive unless I gave it free reign. Fortunately the answer came quickly.

We all tend to think of life lessons as coming one single message at a time, with each standing alone. As well, each single lesson will arrive, of course, at the perfect time to teach us what we need to know about one specific area of our life. In reality nothing is ever that simple.

I have come to realize that each life lesson can also be part of a wonderful jigsaw puzzle connecting with other pieces to create a beautiful picture. They all intersect and they all have multiple sides. Place one piece in the puzzle and it connects with four other pieces.

Each life lesson can have more than one role to fill, offering guidance that holds true in a given moment as well as at a future time. Each one can also combine with other life lessons over time to offer needed insight in new and different circumstances. I mentioned this process in my chapter called, "The Bicycle Story."

The skills I learned through pregnancy and raising my kids ended up having relevance to my journey as a writer. Persistence, acceptance of things I could not change, love, passion and hard work are found in both journeys.

So here you go—"The Paperback Pregnancy." I hope it brings a smile to your face. I also hope afterwards you'll take a moment to think about how this could apply to you. How could lessons from other moments in your life continue to offer you guidance in your journey today?

Don't be surprised if you find many parallels.

The Paperback Pregnancy

After birthing three children, I thought my pregnancy days were behind me. My children are now all adults in their twenties and capable of taking care of themselves. Then one day, out of the blue, I realized the urge had returned. I was now in my fifties. Was it the right choice to embrace pregnancy at this age with all its inherent risks?

Hormones are not easily denied, so I plunged ahead full steam. My husband shuddered. He just wanted peace. Okay, it wasn't a biological baby this time—it was a book.

I began interviewing and writing around ten years ago and over time had accumulated tons of behind-the-scenes material that couldn't be used in a magazine article. I shared these interesting life stories many times and received a great response. What about taking ten of these interviews, writing mini-bios on each person and assembling them in a book?

What I would need to do was increase the word count of each article from 1,000 to around 5,500. I had always struggled keeping within magazines' low word count. How hard could it be? Turns out it was actually very hard. My initial confidence dissolved into a puddle of self-doubt.

One day while driving and thinking about the challenges I was facing, the similarities between trying to write a book and birth a baby came to mind. I couldn't stop laughing. The only difference—this time the gestation period was eighteen months.

While there are accidents, for most of us the road to birthing a baby starts with the joyous decision to build a family. But first you have to know the basics of the birds and the bees. This is lore handed down from parents to children or taught in Sex Ed classes. There are misunderstandings. As proof, I offer the twenty-year-old male who thought if one condom was good, two would be better. Enough said. It was a funny story to share, but the experience was painful.

Unless you have a degree in writing, the process is self-taught with varying degrees of success. The result is many hours spent trying to figure out how to start. Writing a full book would not be like writing a short story, poem or magazine article—I had to produce 50,000 to 100,000 words that stayed interesting throughout and flowed easily. How to begin?

Well, as with pregnancy, you start by trying. Then after a few months with no real progress, you start worrying that it won't happen, that you're not capable. Off you go to the specialist. The pregnancy specialist does tests, gives advice, tells you the odds and offers encouragement. For a writer you might attend an evening class, a writer's group or find a mentor. In the end you head out the door to try again.

No luck? Time for intervention, with a capital I.

In pregnancy that would be IVF—a complicated process. Sometimes IVF takes several tries and it doesn't always work. If successful, you celebrate the news of a growing new life. If not, the decision is made to try again or let go of the dream.

For the truly stuck writer, you might choose a two-day writing workshop or retreat where the book's focus is laid out, title selected, chapters created in bullet points and back cover written. The workshop will plant the seeds of success, but the writer still has to make it happen.

A writer heads home from that workshop to stare at a computer screen. For some this is the end and the dream fades. But for others, the tools learned at the workshop have given them the skills they need and their book starts to take shape. One single chapter emerges—an embryo to build on.

Slowly your pregnancy bump grows (the number of chapters blocked out gets larger) and you begin to get outside encouragement from friends and family. Then you hit another snag. In pregnancy it could be gestational diabetes or other complications that require bed rest. It's disappointing as you want to be out shopping and glowing.

In writing it's the dreaded writer's block rearing its ugly head yet again. Every time someone asks how book writing is going, you want to hide. Deep down you begin to question your talent. This is supposed to be what I am good at! Where is the ease of writing? Where is the joy?

If you're lucky to have a publisher like mine, my "intervention" was a weekly email to set goals and check progress. I still struggled, but that email helped get me to the computer each day.

I love this quote by Ernest Hemingway: "There are days writing is a true joy—but just as many that it is sheer hard work." And that is true for pregnancy as well. You rejoice when feeling your baby kick (each new chapter starts to take shape), but dread the weekly doctor visit to monitor your sugar levels and weight gain (facing the reality of completing your weekly word count).

Then comes the day your labor begins. Sometimes it flows naturally to its ultimate conclusion. Other times it means last-minute interventions—forceps, induced labor, C-section.

For *Life Outside the Box*, which offers ten mini-biographies, that meant last-minute changes from those

I interviewed to make the chapters more accurate, delays getting important needed information, family demands that allowed little time to focus and the list goes on.

It often felt like trudging through mud. You're almost across that elusive finish line. Why can't you get there?

Finally it happens. The doctor hands you that beautiful new baby (the writer hits send and his manuscript is off to the publisher to begin the editing process). It's time to celebrate. The hard work is done—RIGHT?

Much to my surprise as a mother and a writer—this is not true in either case.

As a mother, I had a cold when I delivered my second child, which she of course caught immediately. She could hardly breathe the first few weeks of her life and I spent many anxious moments in emergency. Another of my babies was given the label "failure to thrive." It turned out to be the result of a mild allergy, but that took several months to figure out. Jaundice, colic, lack of sleep, family interference—all are challenges a new parent can face.

As a writer, you face the difficult editing process—much needed, but still hard to embrace. Add to this is final proofing, feedback from distributors, possible changes to cover art, developing a marketing campaign, book promotion and that all-important launch to deal with. Sleep can be elusive as you try to deal with all the demands. The workload is enormous, and it comes at a time when you are truly tired.

In the end, your baby becomes your pride and joy. Nothing beats watching a child sit up, roll over, take that first step, laugh for the first time or say that first word. Why is it never "mama"? I am over-the-moon proud of who my three children have become as adults, but the road from their birth to this moment proved more complicated than I ever imagined.

The same has held true for my journey as a writer. There was nothing like holding the first copy of my book in my hands or sharing my joy with friends and family at my launch.

However, what should have been a six-month process stretched into eighteen-months of highs and lows followed by two years of struggling to learn marketing. It was much harder than I ever expected. I'm grateful I had no idea what I was saying yes to when I first started on this journey.

Would I do it again? Absolutely. There is no denying those hormones that drive us to achieve despite the difficulties. In fact, I intend to embrace at least four or five more literary pregnancies. Hopefully the journey will get easier with each and I will continue to find a better balance between my work and my creative time.

"Life is like a puzzle .... You need all the small pieces to see the bigger picture! This small piece may seem less important but it might actually be a small piece of heaven."
Unknown

Know Your Why

As I was choosing the interviews to include in my first book, I realized I needed to add a few new ones to get the right mix of diverse journeys. I ended up reaching out for interviews with a spoken word poet, a charity founder and the publisher who was guiding my personal author journey—Julie Salisbury. It was strange for me to switch roles from the person being mentored to the interviewer, but well worth the effort.

One of the first things I learned in one of Julie's publishing workshops was to figure out my *why*. Why was it important to write this book? There was a *what* in there too—What was my message? But in the end, *why* took precedence.

When I interviewed Julie, I began to understand not only her personal journey, but the reason she feels it so important for the authors she works with to discover their why.

My publisher grew up as part of the British working class during the Margaret Thatcher years. The strong message drilled into her daily was if you work hard, you can have it all. There was a well-defined checklist to follow—career, marriage, home ownership, travel and pension. When she hit an early roadblock because she hadn't gone to the "right" schools, she forged ahead in a new direction and succeeded, just like Prime Minster Thatcher told her she could.

Product development proved to be her forte. Every eighteen months she was headhunted for a new position and she quickly rose through the ranks. The constant job changes were perfect as they usually coincided with growing boredom at her current position.

By age thirty-five she had the BMW, the luxury home and the well-to-do husband. They entertained business friends, golfed on weekends and did all the things expected of people in their social position. The checklist she was given as a child was complete. She had it all, so she figured she must be happy.

Travel was a big part of Julie's job. She was often on a plane flying from one international destination to the next, staying in a different five-star hotel each night.

One morning she woke up totally disoriented. For a few minutes Julie couldn't remember where she was. Throwing the curtains back she looked out over a scene that would forever be etched in her memory.

There she was, ensconced in a beautiful hotel perched high above the locals, looking down into a rundown street filled with people living in abject poverty. This disconnect hit her like a ton of bricks. What was she doing with her life? She had done what everyone had told her would make her happy. Instead, it had left her confused and empty.

That single moment in time was life-changing. It led Julie to walk away from her life as it then stood and live the next five years as a nomad traveling around the world on a sailboat with an old friend. This must be the life she was meant to have. Unfortunately, one day her traveling companion decided to call the arrangement off.

Lost again, with no new direction, those same questions arose. "Why am I here living this life?" and with that, "What is my purpose?" These two questions walked hand in hand.

It took Julie many years, including another two years sailing with a new beau, to discover the answer. First she wrote and published her own travel book. Then she created a workshop to help others do the same.

As she began leading these workshops, the appreciative comments she received from her students helped her realize her true gift and purpose. Her why is to show others how to share their wisdom through publication,

Julie now clearly understands that her journey has led her to this point, to her *why*. The feedback she was receiving from all the people she was helping also reinforced that she is truly fulfilling her purpose.

Discovering my *why* came about quite differently. My journey as a writer began when I realized my passion for hearing other people's stories could be used in a positive direction. If I was willing to write an article, I could interview to my heart's content and most would share their story willingly. It took several years of interviewing for me to realize I was fulfilling my purpose as well.

I no longer remember the exact moment when I came up with the phrase I mention in my introduction, "It is the journey of real people living real lives that will define our generation." It was a moment of clarity that brought my uniqueness, my passions, my purpose and my *why* all together in one tidy package.

Today I walk firmly along this path. Every interview I do, every time I take the stage to speak, every article or chapter I write, each fulfills what I know is my purpose—the reason I am on this earth. Simply put, I give wings to the stories of others and—with this book—to mine as well.

My hope is that the wisdom found within these stories will offer others the courage to embrace their own uniqueness, to walk their own path without apology and to help them offer that same acceptance to others they meet.

"You are worthy. Your light matters. Your life matters. It's purposeful. It's essential we all play our part in the grand plan. No part is more important than another. Every part is essential. Are you willing to play your part?"
Sue Dumais, Founder of Heart Led Living

"They Were Wrong"

A few years ago, there was a post that went viral on Facebook. Everyone was sharing it. It went something like this, "If you could tell your twenty-year-old self one thing, what would it be?" I remember reading it for the first time and without even thinking typed out in caps—"THEY WERE WRONG!"

I sat back stunned. My heart was pounding and my emotions running high. Where did that come from? Obviously this was important to me.

Over the next week I let this idea have free reign to run in the background as I went about my day. During quiet moments my thoughts would turn toward those three words. Slowly but surely I began to understand the lesson waiting for me.

In earlier chapters I have shared my difficulties as a child. I just didn't fit into the role the world I lived in expected of me and needed me to fulfill.

I was a lovely little blonde girl who was supposed to be a peaceful, loving example of someone embracing the spiritual life. I would love the church and love school. I would learn to play piano and use it to help out with church needs. Most likely there was an unspoken desire that I would grow up to marry a minister—back then, women were only encouraged to be in a supportive role—and continue the family tradition of service to the church, but that's only a guess.

The dream of my being this person was popped early on. My parents instead dealt with an intelligent, intense, impatient, nosy, angry, driven, obviously unhappy soul who didn't fit in even slightly.

Back then little was known about how children might differ. People weren't aware of things like ADD. It was all about training children to fit into the expected mold. If you managed to do that, you were a successful parent and received lots of pats on the back. With no understanding of what was going on, my parents faced a challenge they could not possibly succeed at.

My perspective and expectations were skewed as well. Because there was no knowledge or acceptance of differences among individuals, there was no way for me to understand why I seemed to be different. I thought everyone's mind raced like mine, so I became annoyed with people who didn't seem to be able to follow my train of thoughts. They obviously must not be really listening to me.

There were other times when I decided everyone else must be more complete human beings. I was clearly missing an important ingredient. This thought added a big dollop of self-loathing to my deep well of unhappiness.

Then there are the most hated words in my memory which I heard way too often, "Oh, Marilyn, if only you could just..." This would be shared with a pitying, sad face. I assume they thought it conveyed compassion, but the opposite came through.

The implication inherent in those words was obvious. If I could only change myself to become the person they wanted and needed me to be I would fit in, be loved, be accepted and be happy. All would be right in the world.

I did want that life, but deep down in my core I knew I could never become that person. I wasn't put together that way and the cost of living a lie was too high. Every day I walked with the knowledge that who I was had a negative effect on my father's ministry.

On that momentous day when I responded so emotionally with "THEY WERE WRONG," it validated how far I had come in embracing and celebrating my unique self.

Learning self-acceptance and its companion self-love is a slow journey I have been on for the last decade, and one that still continues today. Up to the point I responded so strongly on Facebook, I had quietly been going through this process in private. Now I had thrown down the gauntlet. It was out there for the world to see. There was no turning back.

Love me, like me, dislike me—no worries. I stand firm knowing the fact that I am not a mistake, nor am I missing an ingredient. I am exactly who I am meant to be and I am fulfilling a purpose that is mine alone.

One day I stumbled upon another concept that pairs well with this one. Fellow author, lawyer and life coach Danielle Rondeau offered me a copy of her book *I Am Enough* to read and review. In it she openly shares her journey as a perfectionist and overachiever. Failure was not an option. Empty time was not an option.

Over the course of the book we follow her roller coaster ride of self-discovery. Time and time again, one layer would be exposed, an answer received and peace would follow. Then the tension would again start to build.

I loved the truthfulness of how Danielle shares her journey and the idea that the answer never comes in a single revelation. We are layers of experiences that need to be explored one at a time, an important life lesson waiting beneath each. Best of all though, I loved her title, *I Am Enough*.

Put the two together and it becomes a strong mantra— an important truth to bring out during moments of self-doubt: "They Were Wrong—I Am Enough!"

Just reading those two statements together resonates deep in my soul. It embodies letting go of those old recordings running through my subconscious filled with negative messages from the past. They are terrible shackles I had allowed myself to be burdened with for far too long.

The statement then moves to what is a deep and wonderful truth. We are all exactly who we are meant to be. There is nothing missing. We are who we are for a reason. We don't have to understand it all; we only need to embrace this important truth.

"They Were Wrong"

Allow yourself to release those negative voices. It's time.
"Why fit in when you were born to stand out?"
Dr. Seuss, Children's Book Author

~

The Art of Mentoring

My issues with a lack of self-acceptance kept me apart from those who would have stepped in as my mentor for many years. I just didn't trust anyone to know and love me for who I was. I mistakenly thought a mentor would most likely try to change me into someone who would fit better into society's cookie cutter mold.

What a loss! It is one of my greater regrets.

At every step along my journey to become a published author, I was constantly put in touch with people who truly desired to help me. This was especially true during the time I was trying to build the magazine I co-owned. I had no idea what I was doing; I was simply swimming as best I could, hoping not to drown.

The market was tough and very competitive. Building a large and diverse readership actually proved very easy for me. On the other hand, building a magazine that was financially profitable was elusive and the long hours were taking their toll. It was obvious to most I was struggling.

At every event, and at every party I attended, I met people who wanted to support our efforts. Some were full of advice about what I should be doing. Many times I already knew most of what they were sharing, but there was only me to do the additional work. We just didn't have the finances to hire a talented staff. What I really needed were more hours in the day.

Then there were those who wanted to guide me in my journey through local industry politics so I didn't make an error in judgement. I will always be grateful to them because it was clear that they loved me and cared about my future. I took to heart and considered each word they shared with me, but that didn't mean I always followed their advice.

From day one I decided fashion politics would never guide my choice as to who would be featured in upcoming issues. I instead chose to let go of the drama and local politics and make decisions based simply on the person's work within the industry. Some of my bolder choices were not popular.

When unsure of a decision, I loved to ask my husband's opinion. He had no industry ties or interest in fashion. I would give him the pro and con facts for inclusion—why a certain person's work justified and article and what the political downside was. His perspective was always unique and I counted on his unbiased observations. He could cut out the politics in an instant and get to the core of the issue. This clarity always made the answer easier to see. I couldn't love him more.

After several years of running the magazine the tables started to turn. While I was still reaching out to my mentors for feedback, I discovered others reaching out to me asking for my guidance. It was unbelievably flattering. I was ready and willing, but first I took some time to go through my experiences and see what qualities were needed.

We all want to share the wisdom we have gleaned during our journey. While this wisdom is usually the main reason someone has reached out to us, we can't expect them to embrace it blindly. Their path will be unique, not a repetition of the one we are on.

The people others need in their life and the choices they need to make will not be the same as ours. There is no perfect road everyone should follow. All we can do is offer our insight for consideration.

Here are a few key points I chose to focus on as I embraced the role of mentor:

- Be honest and nonjudgmental.
- Offer insight without attachment.
- Be sure there is wisdom and experience behind what you share.
- Listen, listen, and listen some more.

There is a lot in those four statements. I encourage you to read them again and let the ideas settle for a bit.

Be Honest and Nonjudgmental

Being honest sounds easy, but it comes with the caveats of love, kindness and a lack of judgment. Trust me, it's harder than you think. If what the person you are mentoring is going through happens to strike an emotional trigger for you, you might find it difficult to be objective.

Your feedback needs to be free of emotional response. You have to separate yourself from knee-jerk reactions and let your inner wisdom come forth.

Offer Insight Without Attachment

The next consideration, and the most important in my opinion, is to give your feedback without attachment. This was hard for those who mentored me. This is hard when I mentor someone else. Their journey is not your journey. Sharing your knowledge is important, but don't expect them to follow it.

The person you mentor needs to process all the input they receive and come up with an answer that resonates with them personally. It will be unique. It will not be the same as your answer, even given the same set of circumstances.

A good mentor needs to be able to step aside and allow the individual to consider everything, to come to their own conclusion by listening to their unique inner voice. I know how hard it can be to let go when the decision made is one you may not agree with, but letting go is just what you need to do.

I am truly grateful for the mentors in my life who have done just this. I know it could not have been easy for them as this is probably the biggest challenge someone stepping into the role of mentor will face. We are asked to give, accept, offer, support, champion and embrace the journey of another whether we can see the results of our influence or not. It needs to be enough that we are meant to be there offering our pieces of gold.

Be Sure There is Wisdom and Experience Behind What You Share

Rather than personal preferences or opinions, bring your knowledge and experience to the table when you respond. What real struggles have you gone through that you can share? How did they affect you? What have you learned from other professionals who mentored you? This is real guidance offered by someone who has walked the same path. Each of us needs to know we are not alone, and that we can come out the other side moving forward toward our dream.

Listen, Listen, and Listen Some More

Lastly, I came to realize the best mentoring mostly involved listening, listening and more listening. As a mentor, you are their sounding board on whom they can try out new ideas. Based on what they share, you offer ideas or perspectives they may not have considered, rather than truths they have to embrace.

You are there to offer emotional support when they are feeling overwhelmed and to share knowledge if they ask for it. Then you are asked to let it all go and respect their personal choices.

Knowledgeable, supportive, non-judgmental, caring, passionate—these traits make for a good mentor.

If you are given the opportunity to offer mentorship, I strongly encourage you to embrace it. In fact, I personally feel everyone should step into the role of mentor at some point in their life. It's an experience like none other and the rewards are priceless.

> *"[Mentoring] is the second most important factor after education in determining a person's professional success."*
> **Korn/Ferry International**

~

Say No to Say Yes

I have mentioned Sue Dumais a few times already. She has proven to be a wonderful mentor and guide for me over the last few years, so it's no surprise I have received several treasures from her deep pockets. Another amazing bit of wisdom she often shares is, "Sometimes a no is a heart-led yes." Perfect.

The strong pull to put others' needs before my own, learned from my upbringing as a minister's daughter, has proven hard to let go of. If someone needed me, I had to act.

When I was a stay-at-home mum this was manageable. However, as I moved into writing and running a local magazine it became much more difficult to fulfill that mandate as I met and worked with more and more people.

Event invites were also hard to turn down. I wanted to fully support the community that had given me so much opportunity, but the number of events I was being asked to cover kept increasing. My calendar was becoming chaotic and hard to manage.

Then I took on a part-time office job. Initially I had agreed to work two days per week, but within six months I had allowed myself to be coaxed into full-time hours. My employer needed me to work more. How could I say no? The next thing I knew I was staying late on Fridays as well.

On top of that I still had my family responsibilities, writing commitments and all the work that came with running a magazine. A crisis of tsunami proportions was building.

Once or twice over this time I hit the wall and melted into a pool of tears. There just didn't seem to be enough hours in the day. Attempts to pass off some of my work to others usually backfired and the responsibility would land back on my desk a week or two later. I loved what I did and didn't want anyone to think I wasn't grateful, but I just couldn't seem to find any balance.

The day of reckoning came when my husband found me collapsed on the bathroom floor, completely exhausted and unable to get up. After making sure I was basically okay, he brought me the phone so I could call in sick to work. I spent the rest of the day stretched out on the couch reconsidering my schedule. Something had to give.

The next day I offered my resignation at the job I was working. I had never intended to be there full-time and they honestly needed someone who could commit one hundred percent. It was hard to give up the paycheck as writing was not bringing in any money. It also hurt that my employer didn't respond well to my decision. But I knew in my heart this was the right move for both of us.

Next I began the very long process of learning how to say no to at least some of the avalanche of invites. Choosing not to attend any event created a feeling of guilt. I appreciated all the opportunities the community provided me and I wanted to support everyone equally.

However, the sheer number of commitments I was asked to make had become far more than I could handle, and each one came with a review I needed to write. The time it took to do each write-up had to be taken out of the time I set aside for my personal writing. I had to come to terms with the fact that this just wasn't possible.

Somehow I had to make a change whether it was popular or not.

One day I felt led to reach out to Sue for guidance. Her response was that I should quiet my mind and just listen. If my heart—my intuition—said yes, then the time and energy will be there to fulfill my obligations. If there is a lack of clarity, stress or a clear no, then that is a "heart-led yes," which means that saying no is the right choice for me personally. My intuition would steer me in the right direction.

I was not letting everyone down by saying no these opportunities; I was focusing on where I was most effective. I couldn't do or be my best if I was stretched too thin.

A year or two later she added the note that every time I said no, I was at the same time saying yes to something else. My focus could be positive—what was it I was saying yes to each time I responded no to a request?

Learning it was okay to say no helped me finally let go of that early mandate of trying to be everything to everyone, but it took a long time for me to develop this conversation with my heart. Some days the answers came quickly and clearly, while other times they proved hard to hear. Sometimes it felt more like having one of those old-fashioned balance scales in my mind. Over the course of several days, the reasons kept adding to one side of the scale until it tipped in that direction, making the choice clear.

Each time you are offered an opportunity or choice, stop for a moment. Try to find a quiet space where your mind is not running the show. Listen to your instincts. Your intellect will always try to move you toward what society and your upbringing says you *should* do. Your heart takes all that information and processes it in a creative way that allows you to see possibilities your mind couldn't conceive.

If you're even questioning whether an opportunity or a new direction is something you should say yes to, it's a clear sign you need to pause and listen. Don't rush. Allow yourself to take whatever time you need to feel the answer resonate—it won't always arrive the minute you ask the question. Trust the process.

Your intuition will offer guidance at a time that is best for your journey. All you need to allow your heart to guide you is patience, a desire to listen and, if the answer is yes, the courage to leap.

"You know, sometimes all you need is twenty seconds of insane courage, just literally twenty seconds of embarrassing bravery, and I promise you something great will come of it."
"Benjamin Mee," Fictional Character in We Bought the Zoo

~

Is Hearing "No" the End of Your Dream?

This is such an exciting chapter to write. We are trained from a young age to believe that if someone says no to us—as we reach for a job, a goal, an idea, a new direction or a dream—then that ship has sailed. It's a final answer. Yet time and time again I've met people who didn't seem to respond to negative feedback or any other kind of roadblock that attempted to end their dream. The word "no" just didn't seem to exist in their vocabulary.

Sometimes they changed it to yes. Sometimes they went around that "no" or roadblock by taking a different path. Sometimes they just didn't seem to recognize the no or roadblock and forged straight ahead. Whatever their response, it didn't involve them walking away.

Have you ever watched one of those Say Yes to the Dress bridal shows? An excited future bride comes in with her entourage ready to find the perfect gown. She is put in a wonderful creation and turns to the mirror. With a huge smile on her face she exclaims, "I love this."

Glowing with confidence, she walks out to show her family and friends only to be shot down. Instantly the smile is gone. Suddenly the only thing she can see in the mirror is what they say is wrong with this choice. Their opinions have changed how she sees herself in the dress.

Whether it comes from your social circle or from a negative inner voice, we've all heard the words "that's not going to work" and "what could you be thinking?" at least once in our life.

Each time it happens in pretty much the same scenario. A new idea or a big dream has exploded into our consciousness. Excitedly we share this with others. But instead of saying "Wow!" and exploring the possibilities with us, all they can see is the negatives—the why nots. As friends they feel obliged to share these thoughts to make sure we know what we're doing.

Our dream pops like a fragile soap bubble and, before for we know it, we find ourselves wondering how we could have been so misguided. The dream fades away.

I talk a bit about this in the chapter on mentoring, but I want to restate it here. What we all need in these moments is a skilled mentor—someone who integrates all the traits of a good mentor. This should be someone who is willing to see the possibilities and potential in our idea. They are there to help us see a path that might make it all possible. They are also there to share the traps that might lie along this path, so that if we choose to move forward, we can embrace it with our eyes wide open.

While your new dream is still an idea, your and your mentor's goal should be one of exploration. Who knows? Perhaps while you are looking at the possibilities from all angles an even better idea will arise.

For me, my racing mind and strong emotional radar often saved me from overthinking my decisions. If my heart says yes, I leap without question or consultation. There are, of course, pros and cons to this way of doing things.

Leaping blindly has led me to some tough times where I had to learn on the job as I tried to meet deadlines, all while in the public eye—not an easy path. However, it has also kept me from walking away from a fabulous opportunity after the naysayers told me all the reasons why it was a bad choice. For that I will always be grateful.

What I have learned over my decade of interviewing is to reach out to my ujamaa circle of friends for feedback. They know what I have accomplished against all odds. They want me to succeed. They are able to offer me safe and positive mentorship, and they bring their knowledge and life lessons to the table. Best of all they will accept and support any direction I take, whether it follows their advice or not.

I still make most decisions quickly, but having my ujamaa circle of friends—my tribe—as a resource at my fingertips gives me a confidence I did not have before. If I do end up learning in the public eye, it is a much easier journey with them by my side.

There are two stories I would like to share with you. Both offer true life examples of how you can be faced with a negative response or what appears to be an insurmountable roadblock, but through hard work and determination still find a way to succeed. No one can stand in your way.

Norwegian perfume designer Geir Ness has been blessed

from a young age with a positive energy and drive that most of us work many years to achieve. From his teen years on, he never let anyone stop him from achieving his dreams. I think he is truly deaf to negative feedback.

While in his twenties, Geir applied for a tourism job on the island of Majorca. The top requirement was you had to speak Spanish—he didn't. Most people would have just assumed that meant they'd receive a no, that there was no point in applying. This was a roadblock to their dream that could not be breached.

Not Geir. He really wanted this opportunity, so he headed downtown to line up along with hundreds of other applicants. When it was his turn he nailed the interview, bringing all the positive energy and charm he possessed into the room.

Geir had a stroke of luck; the person who was to evaluate his Spanish competency had gone out for a few moments. The interviewer was so impressed with this enthusiastic young man that they waived the evaluation and a few days later he was officially hired.

Once on the island he dove in and worked as hard as he could, committing one hundred percent to picking up the language as quickly as possible. He treated each tourist who asked for his help like a VIP, and many responded by writing letters of appreciation to the company. Despite the fact he initially didn't have the specific skills asked for, Geir became such an asset to the company that they promoted him to a management position after only a few months.

The second story is from Warren Dean Flandez, a

Singer-Songwriter who also owns two vocal studios. I met Warren on the runway between shows at Vancouver Fashion Week. Everyone seemed to know who he was. I was curious, but I was there to cover the runway shows so I let it slide.

One season he took time between shows to come over and introduce himself. As I learned more about him, I was drawn to the kindness and joy that radiated out freely from this young artist and entrepreneur. Then I had the privilege to hear him perform live and I was hooked. Warren quickly rose to the top of my must-interview list.

While the official interview took a while to happen, I met him for a one-on-one chat first to see if his story was ready—I often refer to it as "seeing if the soup is cooked." In general, I find a person's journey often doesn't hit its stride until they are forty or so—I offer myself as a prime example. Mine drastically changed directions at age fifty. Warren was only in his early thirties. I was curious, but not ready to commit until I learned more.

That first conversation nailed it for me. I was on the edge of my seat throughout, totally drawn into Warren's journey. This was a story that had to be told now and most likely, it would need to be told again further down the road.

It took several more months, but in the end we managed to get a full interview on tape. Warren was such a good storyteller that when I sat down to write my first article on him the words literally flew onto the page. I wish it were always that easy.

Warren struggled with severe asthma all through his

childhood and teen years. During one particularly difficult time, his mum reached out to his long-time family physician to ask what else they could try. The response was to look into an activity that would increase his lung capacity—his wind.

The two options presented were to take up playing a musical instrument or to try singing. There was no competition in young Warren's mind—singing called to him. However, it didn't start well.

Warren's first vocal teacher was not impressed and after a few lessons told him he didn't have the right DNA, the potential, to succeed. She encouraged him to focus on acting or some other activity. That didn't sit well with the budding artist.

His parents had set a wonderful example on how hard work can bring success and he took that to heart. There was a vocal teacher who ran a local gospel choir, but he wasn't accepting any new private students. This didn't deter Warren who had his eye on the prize.

He joined the choir and wore the director down until he finally accepted him as a student. This new teacher challenged Warren, pushing him harder than he'd ever been pushed before. Despite his asthma, he had to run around outside the church until he was ready to collapse.

Over time his wind and voice developed. He began to perform more, studios hired him for in-house work, he opened a vocal studio and released several albums. In one high moment, he was asked to tour with James Brown. Unfortunately for Warren, Brown passed away before the tour began.

In 2016, Warren released *Eternally Grateful*, a gospel album that quickly received critical acclaim and won several Canadian industry music awards. His vocal school has grown to include two locations and is a positive force for many singers, from young talent just starting out to mature singers wanting to re-embrace their passion. Warren has also used his position to give back to countless charities through fundraising at all school and choir performances. How fortunate he didn't let that first "no" keep him from this incredible journey.

Whether you change direction to go around, climb over or plow through a "no" or a roadblock, don't let someone else tell you that you should walk away. Only you can tell if the direction you're heading is the right one.

If your intuition guides you to walk a different path, so be it. And never forget, if it's saying "Yes" to walking through a door of possibility, that same intuition will also help you find the way.

Have faith and just keep moving forward. Each step will take you that little bit closer to your dream.

"When someone tells me no, it doesn't mean I can't do it. It just means I can't do it with them."
Karen E. Quinones Miller, African-American Journalist, Historian, Author and Community Activist

"The individual who says it is not possible should move out of the way of those doing it."
Tricia Cunningham, Health Care Expert, Life Coach, Speaker, Media Agent and Author

~

Put the Sizzle on the Steak

As entrepreneurship is not my passion, I can only offer what others have shared with me on the subject. It was luxury shoe designer Ruthie Davis who opened my eyes to this truth about business. Her comment during our interview to "put the sizzle on the steak" holds a bit of wisdom that deserves to be explored.

When the opportunity to interview this designer came through my work with a New York magazine, I was beyond excited. It was going to be the cover story in that issue, an amazing opportunity for me. A few years later I was honored to be allowed to include her story in my first book as well.

Ruthie is a truly talented entrepreneur who first made her mark in the industry working for other companies before striking out to develop her own luxury shoe line—Ruthie Davis®. Her unique brand of high-end footwear brought something new to the industry and soon her shoes were being worn on the red carpet by Hollywood royalty.

True to form, I chose not to do a ton of research ahead of my interview with Ruthie. I wanted to be totally unbiased and hear her story without prior expectations. In looking back, I am not a hundred percent sure that was exactly the right approach in this instance, but I dove in with my usual first questions: "Where were you born? What were you like growing up? Looking back, can you remember any moments that pointed to your embracing this career?"

The answer to the last question was yes. She was in love with shoes from a very young age.

Then Ruthie shared her journey working for other companies and how she approached making her mark in each one. Surprisingly it wasn't her design skills she talked about—and she does have seriously fabulous design skills. There were two things she shared as keys to her success.

The first was that she understood the importance of building and working with a great team. This was her main priority every time she took on a new position. When she finally took the plunge and launched her own brand, she took the exact same approach.

The other key point was more personal. Ruthie intimately understood the importance of the "hook," an advertising term that refers to something designed to entice a customer to purchase a product or to sign up for a service. Remember the catchphrase delivered hilariously by an older woman in a 1984 Wendy's commercial, "Where's the beef?" Everyone repeated it.

Creating the right hook can make or break a product's success on the open market. Ruthie knew this was one of her greatest strength, and she used that strength to her best advantage.

A great example of this came early in her career, during her time at Reebok. She took the company's classic white leather runner and, instead of the side window sporting a British flag, she put in an old military-style dog tag sporting a Reebok logo. It sold through the roof. She shared, "I didn't reinvent the wheel; I didn't reinvent the shoe; I just put the sizzle on the steak." Bingo!

Putting the "sizzle on the steak" might sound like it only applies to sales, but I think it can have a much broader application.

Whatever your passion, whatever you choose to do for your work, your enthusiasm needs to come through when you promote it. You need to reach out into the market in an inventive way that catches the consumer's eye. Who wants to hire you or buy what you're selling if it's just ho-hum or a clone of what is already available?

Take some time to think about your passion in a new light. What is it you are trying to achieve? What are your goals? Let your mind get creative and think about unique ways to offer your passion to others. Ask yourself, "What can I do to make my passion stand out in today's market?"

Know deep in your heart that there is no limit to what you might create. It's time to put the "sizzle on your steak."

"You were born to stand out. Embrace it."
Alyssa Vertullo, Actress

~

"I See You"

Believe it or not, Hollywood can step up to the plate and offer life-changing wisdom. I know this because once I was in the movie theater when it happened. The day was December 25, 2009. The theater was an IMAX, tucked into a multiplex in a Los Angeles suburb. The movie was *Avatar* and we watched it in 3D.

Everyone in my family loves well-done animation and we watch almost every animated movie released. I think 3D IMAX is the best way to view this type of movie. The immense screen and great sound system IMAX technology offers really helps to draw us into the story. And somehow, the 3D effect lets the animated images seem more real. The experience feels more like I am watching a regular movie with real actors instead of animated creations.

That holiday season was a strange one. It had been a great year for me professionally. My partner and I had published over twenty online digital editions of our magazine and in October we had released our first-ever print collectible edition.

Personally, though, I was struggling. My mother had passed away in February. My youngest son was in Ireland and my middle daughter in Australia. That left my husband, my oldest son and I alone for the first time ever.

For me the holiday season is all about family coming together, so having my mum and two out of three kids gone left a void in my heart. I decided the only cure for us was to visit my brothers and their families in Southern California.

Off we headed to Los Angeles where my youngest brother lives. My older brother and his family also visit there every Christmas as his wife's family reside in the area. This large family group offered a great distraction that made it easier to bear having two of my own so far away and my mother gone.

Our family tradition is to gather on Christmas Eve, as many years as possible, at my youngest brother's house. Here we would spend a long day together playing games, sharing an amazing meal and enjoying a special group activity my youngest brother secretly dreams up. Each season it is something new.

One year it was a Wii tournament that pitted cousin against cousin and adult against adult. The winner in each category competed for top honors. I am proud to say I won the adult division, but sad to admit I was clobbered by my niece Melissa in the final playoff.

Another year it was a spoons tournament around the large granite island in his kitchen. Laughter was frequent, and we all left at the end of the day with smiles on our faces and our hearts filled with holiday spirit.

Christmas day my brothers spend with their wives' families. When my mum was alive we would hang out with her, or drag her along on an all-day power visit with the grandkids to Disneyland. After she passed away it became a little more complicated.

As there were only three of us that Christmas, we found ourselves ensconced in a hotel room with two queen beds trying to figure out how to fill the day that stretched ahead. Outside it was warm and sunny so we decided to head out first to enjoy a round of miniature golf course, followed by lunch at a fabulous chicken place we'd stumbled across.

Then it was time for what we planned as the highlight of our day. We'd been dying to see *Avatar* and it wasn't yet showing where we lived. We could go home with bragging rights, having seen the movie before anyone else and being the ones in the know.

Although the multiplex was packed, we managed to snag great seats in the IMAX. The lights went out, we put our 3D glasses on, the movie began and then somewhere near the end an emotional moment brought me to the edge of my seat.

Avatar is a stunningly beautiful movie. It might be created by animation and computer imaging, but the plot and the way it is offered are aimed at adults. While the basic premise is one that has been told before in many different incarnations, it was offered in a fresh and powerful way.

Humanity is invading another world, interacting with the aliens through avatars that are run by soldiers lying in hidden chambers. The main character we follow, Jake

Sully, is one of the soldiers who powers an avatar. In real life he is confined to a wheelchair. While in his avatar construct he has the freedom of movement again.

Over the course of the movie, he is drawn deeply into the culture of these aliens through his interactions with one in particular, a female named Neytiri.

Jake develops a great respect for how these aliens live their lives in harmony with the nature surrounding them. This growing compassion takes him out of alignment with the military's goals to take over the planet. The movie's intensity builds from the moment Jake makes a decision to find a way to protect these unique people and their way of life.

Just in case you have not seen this movie, I don't want to spoil what comes next. There is one scene I need to share, however, as this is the moment that struck me to the core.

An avatar access chamber has been secreted in a hidden location. Jake physically travels to it to place himself in his avatar and become part of the rebellion, to help the aliens fight back. However, the location is discovered and his chamber's integrity is compromised. He is dying.

In one truly touching scene, Neytiri finds Jake's chamber and peers in through the small viewing window at this tiny human body she has never seen before. Even though Jake looks nothing like the avatar she knows, she recognizes his spirit and reaches out to him with the most powerful of words I have ever heard: "I see you." I still can't share this scene without getting emotional.

The scenes that follow continue to embrace this idea of

acceptance. Jake in his avatar form and Jake in his human form are embraced by the aliens as one person who is cherished for the spirit within. They recognize the body as just a shell.

For the next six months I drove everyone I know crazy by intently looking them deeply in the eyes and declaring solemnly, "I see you." For me, it continues to be a profound statement to this day.

I had always felt growing up that if the people I met could really see inside me to the strong-willed, mixed-up person who resided there, they wouldn't be impressed. They wouldn't like me. I had to change, at least outwardly, to someone that society deemed acceptable. So I walked through life as an imposter, trying to hide what I thought of as my broken bits.

The idea of someone looking inside, seeing the unique, real me and embracing who I am, as I am, was mind-boggling.

Learning to love ourselves and knowing we are exactly who we are meant to be are just two truths to be embraced. The importance of surrounding ourselves with people who see us clearly and celebrate us exactly as we are is another. Having friends who hold open the door of possibility about who we can become and what we can achieve is yet another. Each piece of gold is an important part of the jigsaw puzzle that is life, leading us along on our journey to self-acceptance.

And what we know for ourselves as truth, we also need to offer to others.

After this realization, my goal became for me to learn to consciously try and see beneath the surface when I meet someone new—to not let outward appearances distract me from seeing the beautiful spirit within. I am to help them understand the concept of wabi-sabi so they can learn to embrace their quirks. And, when led, I am to become part of their ujamaa tribe lifting them up. Most of all, I can hold open their door of opportunity on what their future can hold.

One day this came full circle when I was talking with my mentor Sue. Not knowing the impact it would have on me, she was led to say the words, "I see you." Everything stopped. There were tears. It was a beautiful moment.

"If only our eyes saw souls instead of bodies. How very different our ideals of beauty would be."
Unknown

by Marilyn

Giving Without Expectation

I was fortunate in my fifties to discover I had a doppelganger. Her name is Randi Winter. While our lives and backgrounds are very different, we are often mistaken for each other at events. We also have a shared passion for connecting and mentoring others. I know she always has my back, no matter what challenges I face. I have hers as well.

Over the years she has offered me a lot of sound advice, much of it focused on building success in my career as a writer. Every once in a while, however, it moves into the personal realm. Such was the case when she talked to me about blessings.

While my budget is pretty tight, one day I found myself upset about what I felt was an injustice within my community. When I quieted my mind to hear the wisdom my heart had to share, the answer was clear. I needed to take action. It was time to open my wallet and create a new door to replace the one that had closed for a particular artist.

I had a little money set aside and felt strongly led to offer it for this cause. Time was needed to let the idea simmer for a few days, but in the end my decision ended up being an easy one. My soul's answer was clear. Yes, this was the right move.

What came next was more difficult. Because of my position within the industry, I felt it important to remain anonymous. My budget wouldn't allow me to do this frequently, so there could be ramifications if word got out and I was unable to help other artists in a similar position. I didn't want to face criticism as to why I stepped in this one time or why I don't do this more often.

There was also something very appealing in the idea of being someone's anonymous fairy godmother. It felt right—always a good sign you're headed in the right direction.

In the beginning, the only person privy to my secret was the person I gave the money to. But eventually pressure began to build for that person to reveal my identity. That was not something I wanted, but I understood why it was being asked. The person who benefited wanted to offer their personal thanks.

Wisely I chose my doppelganger to share my secret with. I knew she would have a unique perspective and most likely the perfect bit of wisdom in her pocket just waiting to be shared. I was right.

Randi is Jewish. What she chose to share in that moment was an important principle in her faith that offers guidance surrounding an act of charity—*Tzedakah*. It says that when such an act is offered without recognition, it is considered an extra blessing. This was just what I needed to hear at the time and it solidified that the choice I made to remain anonymous was the right one.

As I was deciding on the chapters to include in this book, that moment in time kept coming to mind. In response, I decided to reach out to my friend and ask her to share in her own words what this principle is about.

While all I was initially looking for was a short overview, her beautiful response really touched me. It shares in more detail than I could have on my own with my limited knowledge, so I share it here in its entirety.

"There are three levels of Tzedakah. First is to give and remain anonymous. The second highest level is to give anonymously to unknown recipients. The highest level of Tzedakah is to give a gift, loan, or partnership that will create opportunity so the recipient is supporting himself instead of relying on the charity of others. It further clarifies the levels by asking if you give freely or grudgingly. Did you give it before or after being asked? These are ways to become a 'mensch,' a truly good person. Studies show that people feel better when given money and, with it, the choice to spend it on themselves or on others. Those who give it to others either as cash or as a gift report much higher personal satisfaction and levels of happiness than those who spend it on themselves.

"The world needs kindness, justice, and righteousness that flows freely and effortlessly to others, far from ego. 'Tzedakah' has a stronger responsibility factor than 'charity,' which has the connotation that it is optional. Charity too often has a whiff of superior benevolence. It is our moral obligation to share what we have. This is not limited to money. Giving of ourselves with our time, expertise, and connections can be

priceless. From this perspective, even the poorest person or the smallest infant can perform acts of Tzedakah. Sometimes a smile is enough to lighten a grieving heart" (Randi Winter, Owner of Passionate Travel and a member of Canadian Hadassah Wizo).

I absolutely and utterly love the concept of Tzedakah as it guides us to ask the important question of why we are choosing to perform an act of charity. Giving from our heart is an act of service to others, a response to an internal voice. We are led to give, so we give.

Giving solely to receive recognition or because it is expected is self-serving. It does not come from a place of generosity or true charity. This guidance helped me stand firm in my decision to give from a place of anonymity.

Tzedakah is not always easy to embrace. We've all been at events that offer recognition to others doing good work. How many times have you sat there wishing that could be you? When you see someone receiving public recognition, such a nomination or an award, it is easy to feel that their work has more merit—that if we don't receive any public recognition, our individual contributions have less value. This is not true.

Any act of charity you embrace has merit simply because your heart led you in that direction. You have been guided to accept this purpose, to step up in this moment and to welcome the responsibility. Fulfilling your purpose is your reward; nothing else is needed.

There is nothing like the feeling you get when you fulfill an act of charity you were led to embrace. Everything the outside world can offer in terms of recognition pales in comparison.

> *"The best way to find yourself is to lose yourself in the service of others."*
> **Mahatma Ghandi, Indian Activist**

The Pronoun Conflict of 2014

This chapter is hard to write as it includes a story I have never shared with my editor—Nina Shoroplova. How will she receive these words? I have no idea. I only hope by this point she will notice I have included tons more pronouns in this manuscript. Hopefully that counts for something.

Does any writer love the editing process? In looking for a quote to end this chapter, it didn't sound like it. The majority of random comments I found in my web search were actually quite negative which surprised me as I know how important working with a good editor is. The process can make or break a book.

I discovered the importance of editing not only through working with Nina on my first book, but in my role as a book reviewer. Within the first ten pages of reading a book, it is often clear whether or not it has received proper editing. Shockingly, many times the answer is no.

We writers love the words we put on paper. To some degree we can step back and find smaller errors, but there is a blindness as well. We know in our hearts what was in our thoughts as we wrote each sentence. The reader does not. Also, there are times what we have written could be taken to have a different meaning than we intended. My editor caught one in this book, thank goodness; I can't think how that paragraph might have been received had she not.

When rereading, it's not always possible to be objective, to let go of what we know we meant to say. It makes perfect sense to us, so surely everyone else will get it. Unfortunately that isn't always the case. Others might read those same words and come to a completely different meaning.

A talented editor does so much more than just look at grammar and punctuation. They look for the flow from one idea to the next, a consistent style throughout and the accuracy and consistent spellings of people, places and events. They help us see other meanings our words may have, especially ones that could be offensive, and they highlight what needs to be taken out when we get too wordy.

My favorite example of how important a great editor can be is a book I was reviewing in which the author shared his life as a government operative. He had a friend do the editing and she actually did a great job overall. There were few mistakes and the story flowed smoothly. What she may not have had the courage to tell him because they were friends as well, was that referring to overweight co-workers at the head office as "water buffaloes" was perhaps an unflattering reflection on him personally.

This side note was self-serving and very offensive. It didn't showcase a funny or intriguing moment, it just highlighted his prejudice when it came to body types. It was also a complete distraction from the very interesting story he was telling. A great editor would have made that clear and his book would have been much better with this removed.

Good editors also judge more elusive concepts such as warmth. Is your book just a repetition of facts? Is the way you shared your story boring, or have you captured the emotion necessary to draw the reader in and keep them glued until the final page?

I had written for ten years and produced over a hundred and fifty articles by the time Nina edited my first book. I went into the editing process confident I knew it all. It turns out I was very wrong.

From the beginning, my writing was mostly focused on interviewing and sharing the stories of others. No matter what media outlet the article was for, I tried to brand the individual in the public's mind by making it personal. I could only share a snippet of their life usually, so I spent a lot of time choosing what personal moment or moments to include.

Because of the focus of my writing, I began to hate the constant use of pronouns like *he, she, him,* and *her* alternated with the individual's name. It was difficult to write a personal piece without those pronouns, but their overuse felt like being constantly poked when I proofed the article.

It bothered me. Then it started to really bother me. Those dreaded pronouns became like fingers on a chalkboard. It was time to change directions.

I spent many hours over the next few years working on

developing a style of writing that was still personal, but avoided the constant repetition of pronouns and names. Over time I made progress and developed a pride in this new writing skill.

One writer who came on staff at the magazine I co-owned was also in school studying to become an editor. We had many interesting discussions. She had the full list of rules that she believed at the time must be followed. I had ideas on how the rules could be bent to achieve a great article. Together we tried to hash out where the balance lay.

One concept in particular I loved to play around with was how to imply a quote without the standard disclaimers—*he said, she shared, they enthused, she shared with excitement, he noted.* When a writer has several quotes in a single article, those introductions can start sounding a bit unnatural and repetitive. I still used them at times when it made sense, but I did learn there were times I could introduce the quote by the way I had written the previous sentence.

Over time I began to embrace this new talent and was utterly pleased when my editorial student gave me her stamp of approval. I was getting the positive feedback I needed and she was enjoying exploring new directions that took her outside the cut-and-dried rules found in her course work.

This all ended when I received my editor's first notes on my manuscript. She loved pronouns—felt they warmed up the article and made it more personal. She asked me to not be afraid of them. My first thoughts can't be repeated here. I had just spent several years learning how to write with fewer of them and here she was telling me to add them back in.

I explained my position. She shared that their absence was taking away from the warmth needed to tell the person's story. Initially I was concerned that we wouldn't find common ground, but eventually I realized I needed to step back and listen with both ears wide open.

The answer that came was a lesson I now take into all areas of my life.

It wasn't important how many pronouns I included. What was important was that she knew there was warmth missing that, if corrected, could take my book to the next level. Once I understood what the lesson was, I could look at our pronoun conflict with new eyes.

As I reviewed each paragraph she pointed out, I stretched as a writer to figure out how I could bring more warmth into it. Sometimes it involved rewriting a sentence or two, while other times I actually did need to add in more pronouns. There were even instances I had to rewrite the whole paragraph.

Whatever direction felt right, whatever solution I chose, what I discovered was these changes made the passage I was working on so much better than my original.

That lesson led me to reevaluate other areas of my life. There was an inherent guilt when I didn't follow a mentor's recommendations or when friends offered advice I did not follow. It was time to let that guilt go.

When the universe brings someone with wisdom into our lives, listening is important. These mentors have felt the call to offer us gold from their pockets to ease our journey. We need to trust there is an inherent truth meant to guide us in this moment and open wide the doors to our creativity as we explore the truth they have offered us.

All we need to do is listen without judgment, then hold our mentors' words front and center while sinking into that quiet space within. Our intuition is always there waiting, ready to show us the way.

Thank you, Nina, for all your hard work and guidance. I hope we will walk hand in hand for many years.

"A good editor is like tinsel to a Christmas Tree ... they add the perfect amount of sparkle without being gaudy."
Bobbi Romans, Author

~

You Are Ready—The World Is Ready for You

Self-doubt can be such a crippling thing to deal with. I know as I have struggled with it for so long.

The gratitude I feel for all the individuals whose words have guided me in my journey to self-love is enormous. Each and every one has made a difference in my life. Each bit of wisdom they freely shared added to what I knew and offered a stepping stone to what was still to come.

In late spring 2017 I was starting to get really frustrated with my lack of progress in writing. It had been two years since I had released my first book and my new one just wasn't coming together. I tried making a verbal commitment to my publisher, but the date soon passed with only a small amount of progress made.

Procrastination, doubt, writer's block—whatever was happening caused me to question my future as an author. I had the skills. I had the passion. My heart was saying yes. What was holding me back?

One chapter would flow onto the page and the next would stall midstream. My wonderful tribe of close friends stepped in offering the supportive advice that I needed to be patient. There was a reason for this delay. I needed to pause, listen and let this journey unfold at the right time.

Piece by piece I tried to let go of the guilt I felt over this "failure" and instead explore what might be going on in the background. Was there a reason I was feeling this disconnect? Was there something I needed to learn or an important interview that needed to happen before I could move forward? The answer proved elusive.

It was time for a fresh perspective, so I reached out to my mentor during a weekly Heart Led Living call-in session and shared my frustration that, despite all my growth over the last year, I still could not seem to write from a place of calm and joy. Was there any insight she could offer?

Her response that day opened my eyes to a beautiful truth that was just what I needed to hear in that moment. She shared that when connecting with me she saw birds flying—wings and more wings. I was ready to fly.

Then Sue added another truth that hit me profoundly— the world was ready for me. It was time to take the training wheels off. Time to let go of self-doubt and step into my purpose. I am here for a reason and I need to embrace it fully.

I sat very quietly for a few minutes to allow her words to fully sink in and in that silence, my inner voice offered a clear message—there was another book I was meant to write first, *The Wisdom of Listening : Pieces of Gold From a Decade of Interviewing and Life.*

The Wisdom of Listening is a passion project, one that I thought I would only allow myself to write as a reward for completing the book I was currently working on. The idea of doing it first created a huge shift in the well-laid plans I thought were set in stone.

Even once this truth was placed firmly in my hands, I wasn't ready to fully embrace the change. Instead I decided to just sit down at the computer and lay out the bones of this book—title page, possible chapter titles, back cover blurb—so it would be ready to go as soon as I finished the manuscript I was already working on. My assumption was this would quiet the voice urging me forward. However, as soon as I started to lay it out I knew there was no turning back.

Words began to pour out. I couldn't hold back the flow and found myself passionately drawn to write from the moment each day began until late in the evening. It was a completely different experience from the first time around when I struggled daily with self-doubt.

Even though I missed four days of writing to a cold and didn't write on weekends, I finished the first very rough draft in three weeks—a record for me. Not once did I face doubt or the dreaded writer's block.

When I let go of the agenda my head was dictating and fully understood the guidance of my heart, the inner struggle began to ebb and the flying began. Let's face it, how can you fly if you don't know what direction you should be heading?

It is so much easier now for me to embrace the wisdom Sue shared with me that day. I am ready and the world is ready for me. However, this lesson is one that will most likely take me many years to fully integrate.

I have met and interviewed some people who exude confidence. It is truly a gift. But I have also listened to many who, like me, find self-confidence as elusive as a hummingbird—not easy to discover and even more difficult to grasp. If this is a challenge you also face, just know you are not alone. That for many of us, we move towards this goal one baby step at a time.

All through this book I have shared many, many small bits of knowledge that can offer guidance on how to learn to bring self-acceptance and self-love into your life. It can be achieved, but you have to be patient.

Start with focusing on what you love about yourself for just one moment. Follow that moment with another. Slowly build up to an hour of self-acceptance, then a day, then a week. Practice until it becomes second nature.

We are all here for a reason. There is only one of us and each of us has a unique role only we can fulfill. Each of us is irreplaceable. It's time to step into our purpose. We are ready and the world is ready for us.

"Confidence does not come in a handy little package at birth, along with the color of your eyes and the size of your hands."
Julie Chung, Personal Finance Professional

~

"I Am Not My Father's Son"

Two weeks after I finished a rough draft of this book, I headed to New York for a much-needed solo vacation. My husband was off scuba diving with a friend and I had just finished two crazy, busy weeks that left me exhausted. I couldn't wait to jump on that plane.

I love visiting this amazing city. New York is filled with museums and galleries, cool places to visit, wonderful walks, delicious food establishments, hidden treasures, fabulous architecture—my list could go on forever.

If you're traveling solo don't worry; you're never alone here unless you want to be. Whether riding the subway or walking the streets, interesting people are all around you and most are willing to connect.

This was my second trip to New York and I decided from the beginning to focus my daily outings on things I missed the first time around. The first item at the very top of my bucket list was to see a play on Broadway.

With so many to choose from it was hard to decide. I narrowed it down by deciding on a price range I was comfortable with. I also wanted to see something upbeat and funny, and it had to have a matinee available so I wasn't returning home alone late at night.

After changing my mind several times, I eventually settled on *Kinky Boots*. I had missed seeing this award-winning musical when it came through Vancouver so knew it probably wouldn't be back for several years. Also, several trusted friends gave it a huge thumbs up. In the end it proved to be the perfect choice.

While this play is a comedy, there are several touching moments scattered throughout. One in particular seemed to be written for me personally. The main character of Lola is a drag queen (referred to as "she" when in drag) whose father is disappointed his son is not a "man's man." Lola shares her pain with another lead character, Charlie, during a poignant moment that includes the song, "I Am Not My Father's Son." Phrases such as "I'm not the image of what he dreamed of," "the best part of me was what he couldn't see," and "[I] couldn't … mirror what was not in me" rolled out over me like an emotional tidal wave. I am not sure how the rest of the audience responded, but I began to cry quietly.

As I share in the chapter "My Story," I also did not fulfill the vision my parents had for me. It is impossible to explain the impact this has on someone who has not experienced it, but the scars go deep. Although I have grown to fully love and embrace who I am, a part of me will always wish my parents could have found a way to find joy in who I was born to be.

Hearing this song and the reaction it brought was a reminder of that sorrow, but it also allowed me to celebrate how far I have come on my journey to self-love. I let the emotions freely wash through and then settled back to enjoy the rest of the show.

If you also struggle with a family who is disappointed in who you are, the beliefs you hold or the life choices you make, just know you are exactly who you are meant to be. You can take my word on this one. There are no mistakes.

Choose first to cherish yourself just as you are and then reach out to others who will do the same. Offer them the same acceptance. Create a community of friends based on unconditional love and support, and nurture those connections.

These messages are scattered throughout the chapters in this book and are ready to be reread any time you need a reminder.

Remember, family isn't always about blood relations. It's about choice as well.

> *"If they don't like you for being you, be yourself even more."*
> **Taylor Swift, Singer/Songwriter**

~

Do You Know Who You Are?

The idea I want to share in this chapter is hard to pin down in terms of where it originally came from. Looking back, there were echoes of this theme that popped up randomly along the way. My best guess is that it began with Deepak Chopra.

Three to four times a year, Deepak runs a twenty-one-day free guided meditation series, each with a specific theme such as Creating Abundance and Making Every Moment Matter. If I am home I always participate.

At least twice over the years, one day has focused on one specific exercise. We are asked to take a deep breath, release it and then quietly ask ourselves, "Who am I?" Next, we're to pause and repeat the exercise. Then Deepak guides us to listen for our inner voice. What answer bubbles up?

In 2017, this question found a new voice for me in the film *Moana*. As I shared in the chapter "I See You," I love animation and couldn't wait to see this new movie on the big screen at the theatre—the best way to view any animation in my opinion.

What floored me several times as I watched was when the question arose, "Do you know who you are?" It echoed the similar question in Chopra's meditation series.

Moana was asked, "Do you know who you are?" by her grandmother to entice her to learn the heritage that had been hidden from her. At the end of the movie, Moana asks her monstrous enemy Te Ka the same powerful question. I can't say more in case one of you hasn't seen it yet, but that moment brought home the message of the entire movie for me.

I left the theater profoundly affected and continued to ponder the film's impact on me for several months. Who am I? Do I know who I am?

Humanity often answers this question by embracing common labels. We choose to define ourselves by our racial heritage (I am African American, I am Indigenous). There also religious affiliation (I am Catholic, I am Muslim), gender (I am female, I am male), political party (I am a Democrat, I am a Republican), sexual orientation (I am bisexual, I am homosexual) and career (I am a lawyer, I am a nurse).

The small boxes we choose to place ourselves in are endless. While not necessarily negative by themselves, they can create a negative situation—an us-versus-them mentality—that pushes us away from others not like us.

Over the last twelve months, I have tried my best to let go of the boxes society offers as they have not served me well. I stilled my mind through meditation and then asked the question, "Who am I?" What I was looking for were the elements from which I am made. The answer when it came was not simple. In fact, there were many answers. Here are a few:

- I am intuitive.
- I am blessed with a racing mind that is sometimes a hindrance.
- I am emotional.
- I am a passionate interviewer.
- I am driven to give wings to the stories of others.
- I am creative.
- I am strong.
- I am a mentor for others.
- I am loyal.
- I am meant to pass on the wisdom others share with me.

Notice: not once did any of society's boxes mentioned previously appear.

I can work with each of these elements—my elements—and use them to bind myself to others, no matter how different they are. This list is freeing because it is pregnant with possibilities. There is no limits to how I can use these traits and where they will take me.

Do you know who you are? I encourage you to set aside a few moments every day, starting today, to quiet your mind and ask yourself, "Who Am I?" Your analytical mind will want you to embrace the standard answers that separate you from the rest of humanity. Let that voice fade away. Continue in that quiet space, repeating the question until you hear your own inner voice answer.

The truth will connect you to humanity in a positive way. It will help you embrace self-love and give you the courage to stand apart. Knowing who you are will provide a solid foundation for you to stand on and help guide you to your dreams.

"Knowing yourself is the beginning of all wisdom."
Aristotle, Greek Philosopher

~

Sometimes We Can't Understand

I struggled for quite a while trying to decide whether to include this chapter. I was worried I wouldn't be able to clearly communicate this idea, or that I might even get some part of it wrong. It's difficult to explain, and the possibility of people misunderstanding is high.

In the end I had to trust my instincts that it merits inclusion for a reason.

Growing up I believed that we could truly and fully understand another person's journey and pain if we just listen. There would be parallels in our own life that would help the process. It was a naive point of view and one that comes from a life of privilege.

What I have come to realize is that many times, someone else's journey is just too far removed from mine for me to get more than a glimpse into their world. That flies in the face of everything I was brought up to believe; so it took me a long time to even begin to open the door on this wisdom. Every time it arose I would push it back down.

I grew up surrounded by white privilege. When I had boyfriends of another ethnicity, I really thought at the start that I could understand how they experienced each day. I was wrong.

One boyfriend was stopped and questioned by police for running across a street after buying a pair of shoes. Under his arm was a bag filled with just a single shoe box. This isn't the most threatening picture no matter how you paint it so the question arose, "Why?" The answer was because there had been a robbery a few blocks away and his skin was black.

It didn't matter that the description of the perpetrator started with the word "Caucasian." It only mattered that the police were biased by their upbringing to "see" a black man running across a street as someone who was potentially fleeing the scene of a crime.

How could I possibly understand what it felt like to go through each and every day with this bias always looming and ready to strike?

This "suspicious until proved otherwise" treatment of minorities has been a reality throughout human history, but the depth of it was hidden from us in the past by a lack of coverage in the media. With the advent of the internet, we now hear about new injustices daily. Case after case is brought to light. People have died simply because they were feared for their racial or religious identity.

On the world stage there are places where violence and death are constant threats. Safety is unknown—rape, instability and fear are ever present. Children are forced to become soldiers and corrupt legal systems offer no protection. For some people this is their daily life.

It is impossible to understand the reality of living in their world from our safe, North American, suburban home.

We cannot walk in their shoes. It's time to let go of the idea that we can understand and speak for those living a life that is foreign to us. However, that doesn't mean we are powerless.

Passionate people who come together can create a mighty voice that cannot be silenced. We as human beings need to stand together as one and say no to discrimination, war, genocide and suppression. Our collective voice can create change.

When I think about this subject, I am always reminded of the concept of the butterfly effect. This theory states that even an incredibly small, localized change can have large effects elsewhere. Taken to the extreme, this means the simple action of a butterfly flapping its wings in New Mexico can start a chain reaction of events that lead to a hurricane occurring in China.

It may take a very long time, but if the butterfly had not flapped its wings at just the right point in space and time, the hurricane would not have happened.

In addition to adding our voice, holding a safe place for those who stand up to injustice is also important. There are many who love the status quo. For them, change is not desirable and they will push back through intimidation and, at times, with violence. We need to be ready and willing to protect those with the courage to share honestly and publicly about the injustices they face.

What I have come to feel is that the most important thing we can do to create change is to make sure those who have no voice are given a stage to speak from. The world needs to hear their story, their truth, shared from the depths of their real and personal life experience, in their own words and without judgment. It is their story to tell.

We need to hand the brush and paints over to the artist and let them create an image filled with their reality. It is not for us to try to explain that which we have not experienced.

Lastly, we all need to clearly hear what those suffering have to say about what needs to happen to solve the issues they face. Any solutions embraced should be developed in full partnership with those whose lives will be affected. We need to step back and see the solution through their filter.

It's too easy to come in from the outside and try to make shifts based on our values without taking time to understand the needs of those touched the most.

There is a commonality that runs through us as human beings. We all desire love, community, family, health, joy, connection and self-worth. We are also millions of unique spirits walking our own paths—some of them very difficult ones.

Instead of fearing voices that share what we cannot understand, choose today to embrace the truths found in the words of others, and help make sure their voices are given a platform so they can be heard.

"Our lives begin to end the day we become silent about things that matter."
Martin Luther King, Jr., American Baptist Minister and Activist

"Everyone has their own story and that's something I hope for everyone to learn at a young enough age. Just because something is right for someone else doesn't make it right for you."
Hayley Williams, Singer-Songwriter

Diversity Is Our Greatest Strength

Starting about three years ago, on the first of January I would take time to pick a theme for the year. One year my theme was "cherish." Another I believe was "self-acceptance." In 2017, my heart offered up "celebrating diversity." Perfect timing. I hope that over the many chapters in this book you have come to understand that this theme is absolutely one hundred percent in line with my passion.

From 2016 to 2017 the world experienced some major shifts globally. I grew up in the 1960s and 1970s, years of incredible change. As time passed I came to believe society was making progress in embracing these changes and accepting personal differences. The issues of women's rights, racial tolerance and protection for the LGBT community seemed to be receiving wider support. Then suddenly it all began to move backwards.

I am heartbroken as I hear about the increasing violence directed toward minority groups. The growing stories of individuals being dealt with unjustly by immigration officials set off alarms. Words such as "let's make America white again" and accounts of ethnic people born in the US being told to go home break my heart.

People seem to have forgotten that most of our families at one point—whether in this generation or a previous one—arrived in the country they now reside in from a different place. The only exceptions would be a country's Indigenous people.

Why is the world struggling to understand that embracing diversity is desirable? Why is everyone afraid of those around them who don't look, think, act or worship the same? Doesn't each person want to be embraced and loved for who they are? I know I do.

It took me a long time to embrace my own uniqueness, and I was only able to do this because other unique people shared their lives with me.

I grew up in a strict, religious environment that required everyone to think, act and believe exactly the same. My soul cried out for freedom. In the end I rejected that upbringing and have tried to move through life in a way that encourages diversity and acceptance.

When I interview, I do my best to step into each person's world and embrace their beliefs without judgment. That simple act has changed my life completely and helped me grow.

This didn't change who I am deep inside or what I personally believe. Embracing what they share simply helps me to open my eyes to other truths and guides me along in my own journey to becoming the best person I can be.

Look back over the history of the human race. It's those with the ability to think outside the box and look at the world around us in different ways who have moved us forward. Imagining what might be possible has helped to create the life we enjoy today. As soon as we limit those dreams we begin to stagnate.

You don't need to understand or embrace the same ideals as anyone else, and you don't have to walk the same path. Having diverse voices in your world will influence you. It won't change the core of who you are. We are all guided down a path determined by what we personally need to learn.

Once we truly understand and embrace humanity's diversity as its greatest strength, it will change every single aspect of our lives. To quote Wu Hongbo, Under-Secretary General of the United Nations Department of Economic and Social Affairs, "Where ethnic or religious groups live side by side in harmony, diversity can spur creativity, learning, and innovation."

Fear fades and is replaced by the joy of discovery. Our world grows larger and becomes so much more interesting. Diversity allows us to move forward during difficult times and to adapt to challenges we never expected in creative and surprising ways. It binds us together as one voice and with one voice, we can achieve great things.

I challenge you to welcome new friends into your life who do not hold the same political, religious and personal beliefs as you do. Let your discussions be open and free of judgment. Embrace friends from a different faith or sexual orientation. Learn to see the world through their eyes whether you agree with what you see or not. Offer to others what you want to receive—acceptance and respect for who you are and what you believe.

There is no better closing to this chapter on celebrating diversity than this quote from Apple's Think Different Campaign. I share it often and read it any time the feelings arise of being out of step with those around me.

"Here's to the crazy ones, the misfits, the rebels, the troublemakers, the round pegs in the square holes, the ones who see things differently. They're not fond of rules. And they have no respect for the status quo. You can quote them, disagree with them, glorify or vilify them. About the only thing you can't do is ignore them, because they change things. They push the human race forward, and while some may see them as the crazy ones, we see genius, because the ones who are crazy enough to think they can change the world are the ones who do."
Apple's Think Different Campaign

~

Closing Notes

Writing *The Wisdom of Listening* has been an amazing journey, one I knew in my core would happen from the moment artist Pamela Masik shared the idea of her art being a piece of gold in her pocket she could use to help others.

While I thought I would write this book further down the road, I now realize this is exactly the perfect time. My pockets are filled to the brim and overflowing. It is time to give each piece of gold the wings it deserves.

My personal reason for writing this book is simply to pay forward all the wisdom freely shared with me. If any has found its way into your pockets, I encourage you to do the same—pay it forward. There is someone out there just waiting for you to hand them the knowledge they have been searching for.

The opposite is also true. Life has someone out there waiting to share their wisdom with you. It could be the person in front of you at the grocery store or a motivational speaker on stage. You just never know who might hold the knowledge that will provide an answer to one of your questions.

Life is meant to be an amazing adventure full of surprises

and opportunities. All you need to do is take that first step, and then just keep putting one foot in front of the other.

Be fearless. Be accepting. Be open. It's time to grab the handle on your door of possibility and throw it open wide.

Then hold on tight, because the universe is in charge and what lies ahead promises to be an interesting and wild ride.

Dear Readers

I can't thank you enough for taking the time to read *The Wisdom of Listening: Pieces of Gold from a Decade of Interviewing (and Life)*.

This book was easier to write than my first—it literally poured itself onto the page—but it has been harder to put out there as it shares so openly my own struggles to reach a place of self-acceptance.

As an author, I would love to receive any feedback you'd like to share with me, either through a book review or an email. Also, feel free to pop by my website—www.marilynrwilson.com—and sign up to receive news on upcoming books and appearances.

If you're interested in having me a part of an upcoming event you are running, just send me a short email with the details. I'll get back to you as quickly as possible to arrange a time to connect by phone.

I am also happy to support book clubs in any way I can, especially if it means dropping in for a visit – if I'm in the area – to answer questions about my books or about writing in general. If I can't be there in person, we can always organize a Skype appearance.

With gratitude,

Marilyn R. Wilson

Published Titles by Marilyn R. Wilson

Life Outside the Box: The Extraordinary Journeys of 10 Unique Individuals, First Edition

Life Outside the Box: The Extraordinary Journeys of 10 Unique Individuals, Second Edition

The Wisdom of Listening: Pieces of Gold from a Decade of Interviewing and Life

~

Coming soon

Life Outside the Box #2
Behind the Seams

Olio by Marilyn ebook series

Olio by Marilyn: A Bit of Everything
Olio by Marilyn: Notes from the World of Fashion
Olio by Marilyn: Let Me Introduce You To ...
Olio by Marilyn: On a Lighter Note

Author Biography

Marilyn R. Wilson is a freelance writer and speaker with a passion for interviewing. Her career as a writer began in an unusual way: by answering a Craigslist ad. The world shifted when she conducted her first interview—she had found her passion. Since 2006, she has interviewed over a hundred and fifty people from as near as her hometown of Vancouver, Canada, and as far away as South Africa.

Whether through a random encounter on the New York subway or via a one-on-one interview with an internationally recognized artist, her goal is the same—to give wings to the unique journeys of inspiring individuals. In 2007, this goal led the author to co-launch a successful, innovative magazine focused on articles about professionals working in the fashion industry paired with photography and illustrations by local artists.

In 2015, Marilyn took her passion to a new audience with the release of her first book—Life Outside the Box

—the first in a new series highlighting the journeys of real people living extraordinary and real lives.

Social Media Links

Freelance Writer | Published Author | Speaker

Website
www.marilynrwilson.com
Blog
www.oliobymarilyn.com
LinkedIn
www.linkedin.com/in/marilyn-r-wilson-117b6210/
YouTube
www.youtube.com/channel/UCZx-WR1Qzs7MUkXQ1HgipLg
Instagram
@marilynrwilson
Facebook
www.facebook.com/MarilynRWilsonWriter/
Twitter
@oliobymarilyn